DK GARDEN GUIDES

ROSES

RICHARD ROSENFELD

**LONDON, NEW YORK,
MUNICH, MELBOURNE, DELHI**

Series Editor Helen Fewster
Series Art Editor Alison Donovan
Art Editor Ann Thompson
Designer Rachael Smith
Editor Jane Simmonds
Managing Editor Anna Kruger
Managing Art Editor Lee Griffiths
Consultant Louise Abbott
DTP Designer Louise Waller
Media Resources Lucy Claxton
Picture Research Juliet Duff
Production Controller Mandy Inness

First American Edition, 2004

Published in the United States by
DK Publishing, Inc.
375 Hudson Street
New York, New York 10014

04 05 06 07 08 10 9 8 7 6 5 4 3 2 1

A Cataloging-in-Publication record for this book
is available from the Library of Congress.

ISBN 0-7566-0355-2

Color reproduction by Colourscan, Singapore
Printed and bound in Italy by Printer Trento

Discover more at
www.dk.com

Gardening with roses

ROSES CAN BE GROWN in a fantastic range of gardens, from formal to wild. They can be used as manicured, elegant shrubs or as standards, with globes of flowers at the top of single, upright stems. They make superb stand-alone features in the middle of a lawn and gap-fillers in borders, as well as excellent flowering hedges. Climbers and ramblers can be let loose into the tops of trees. And you have a choice of eight different flower shapes, including tight, petal-packed balls ("pompons") and the stylish "high-centered" with a sharp tip in the middle.

When compiling a list of "must-have" roses, make sure that each has a different feature. For good scent, try GERTRUDE JEKYLL or 'Fantin-Latour'. You can even choose a quick color-change rose, like *Rosa* x *odorata* 'Mutabilis'. The flowers start copper-yellow, change to pink, and end up copper-crimson, and you get all three colors simultaneously because new buds keep coming. If you have room, go for *Rosa sericea* subsp. *omeiensis* f. *pteracantha*. Its pointy thorns are flat, red, and translucent. But the most important point when choosing a rose is to match its shape, vigor, and behavior to the style of your garden design

Roses in small capitals (for example, KENT) denote recognized trade names used by rose suppliers.

◀ HERITAGE **brightens up** borders with its lemon-scented, light pink flowers.

▶ **Choose roses** with excellent hips because they add bright colors after the flowers.

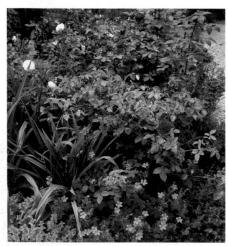

A deep pink rose mingles well with *Geranium* x *oxonianum* 'Wargrave Pink'.

Right rose, right garden

Formal gardens invariably need well-behaved roses with a balanced shape (or ones that can be pruned to keep them orderly) and a uniform height when grown in blocks, while cottage gardens are best for roses with a wilder, more rampant look that adds to the hazy, meandering flow. And in both formal and informal gardens, all sorts of roses can be grown among perennials and other shrubs as dominant, eye-catching features or exceptionally useful fillers. The day of the dedicated rose garden might be over, but as a combination plant it can't be beaten.

Colorful divides

Rose hedges or divides can also be used in formal and informal gardens, and the choice of plants is huge, from knee-high bushes for small areas to head-high shrubs for large spaces. Alternatively, try climbers with a long flowering season trained along horizontal wires fixed to sturdy wooden posts, first checking that the roses' growth statistics roughly coincide with the size of the screen.

Groundcover, standard, and climbing roses

Groundcover roses rarely completely block out the weeds, but they do shoot outward at a low height, and are fun at the edge of a pond or spreading down a bank in a wild garden.

Standards go the opposite way, creating a ball of flowers on top of a long, thin leg. They can be used to encircle a pond, stand at the back of

This subtle blend of colors uses *Rosa* PAUL SHIRVILLE and sky blue love-in-a-mist.

Climbing roses and vines combine to create an elegant and colorful walkway.

Small-scale gardening

Plenty of roses can also be grown in tubs, half-barrels, large pots, and in decent-sized gaps in patios. The smallest roses are called patio or miniature roses, with the miniatures generally being up to 18in (45cm) high, and the patio roses slightly taller. Usually airy and twiggy, they need a small-scale design where they can be seen clearly.

The standard *Rosa* 'Little White Pet' provides a gentle focal point with its ball of flowers.

Pruning

Whichever roses you buy, do not be alarmed by the pruning. You can be as fussy or relaxed as you like. Some roses have even survived sessions with a hedge trimmer and still performed incredibly well. But you must always get rid of the three Ds: the diseased, dead, and damaged wood. After that, tailor your regimen to match your and your roses' needs and your garden design. For a neat look, prune bushy roses hard, to whip them into shape. In cottage gardens, a skimpy trim is fine. You decide what goes.

a border, or mark the beginning of a very grand path, and they keep the eye moving around.

But for the best aerial show, you need climbers and ramblers. For the ultimate climber, try *Rosa mulliganii*, a rampant wild white rose. And try one with a beautiful high-pointed flower, like 'Guinée'. The color is a deep, dark red, and the rich scent goes straight to the head.

Patio roses are ideal for tubs, and create a superb show with busy Lizzies.

Types of roses

OVER CENTURIES OF CULTIVATION, roses have been divided into types according to how they grow, when they flower, and how they need to be pruned. Knowing the characteristics of each type helps you choose which you need—from a modern, long-flowering rose for a formal border to a wild rose for easy growth in an informal garden.

Old garden roses

There are many different kinds of old garden roses. They vary enormously but generally have one superb flowering period in midsummer, many with a fantastic rich scent and strong color. They can be grown in borders or as feature plants.

◀ Alba rose
A typical Alba rose, *R. x alba* 'Alba Maxima' is a free-branching, large shrub with hardly any prickles and a midsummer burst of flowers. Albas are good hedge and border plants, and need minimal attention.

▶ Bourbon rose
Bourbons like 'Zéphirine Drouhin' are vigorous, with more than one summer show of flowers, usually good scent, and a large, open shape. The stems are smooth or prickly. They are ideal in borders, against a fence, or as hedges.

◀ Gallica rose
The arching 'Complicata' has one excellent display of scented flowers. It belongs to the oldest group, the Gallicas, with thorny stems, a robust constitution, and a short, bushy spread. Grow Gallicas as a hedge or in beds.

Wild roses

Also known as species roses, they invariably have one flowering period and are often perfect for hedges or for growing up into trees. They require very little attention.

▲ *R. xanthina* 'Canary Bird'
With the look of a wild rose, *R. xanthina* 'Canary Bird' has single, five-petaled blooms followed by blackish hips, and arching growth up to 10ft (3m) high. Wild roses are ideal in cottage gardens.

Modern roses

Many types of roses are included within the modern rose group, all giving a flowery display that just keeps coming from summer to autumn. The larger, bushier kinds can be grown in rows to make hedges, garden divides, and even impenetrable barriers. There are also lower-growing groundcover types, and miniature or patio roses that look good in pots.

▲ Large-flowered bush rose
DUBLIN BAY can be grown both as a large shrub and as a climber, and has a long flowering period.

▲ Cluster-flowered bush rose
'Southampton' has the typical look of a cluster-flowered bush rose, with a mass of flowers.

▲ Shrub rose
Shrubs are a diverse group. 'Little White Pet' can be grown as a standard or a compact shrub.

Climbing and rambling roses

The key difference between climbers and ramblers is that climbers usually have stiffer stems, and they can be trained into a strong framework from which their shoots develop. They are better on walls than ramblers, which fire up long, flexible stems from the base, making them easy to train up arches, pillars, and pergolas—they can even climb into trees. Ramblers tend to have smaller flowers in summer clusters.

▲ Climbing rose
'Danse du Feu' has 8ft (2.5m) of stiff growth, and is ideal for flowering against a modest wall.

▲ Rambling rose
'Bobbie James' is best trained into a sturdy old tree, and has a mass of creamy white flowers.

Choosing roses

ROSES ARE SOLD IN POTS or bare-root (usually from mail–order companies). The container–grown kind can be planted at any time, even in summer. Check their health when buying, and reject the diseased and feeble. Bare-root roses have been dug up from growing fields in the dormant season for planting as soon as possible.

Even covering of flower buds

Glossy, healthy-looking leaves

Strong, healthy topgrowth

Container-grown rose
Check that the plant has vigorous stems and a good shape. The soil should be moist and firm. Also look for healthy roots that are not congested.

Sparse foliage

Diseased leaves

Bare-root rose
Look for well-placed shoots and sturdy main roots to anchor the plant in the ground, along with plenty of smaller, fibrous ones.

Strong joint between roots and stems

Weak shoots

Thick cluster of strong roots

Spindly roots

Planting bare-rooted roses

Plant as soon as you can, in late autumn or early winter, but not in waterlogged or freezing soil. When delays happen, keep the roses cool and frost-free, occasionally standing the roots in a bucket of water. Before planting, soak the roots for one hour and prune any dead, diseased, or damaged wood, and any crossing stems. Also trim back any damaged roots to healthy tissue. Finally, dig a wide hole that is deep enough to take the roots comfortably, and fork in plenty of well-rotted organic matter to get the roses off to a good start.

Fill in soil, firm down, and water area well

Check the planting level
Make the planting hole deep enough for the joint between the roots and stems to be 1in (2.5cm) below soil level. Check using a cane placed horizontally.

Removing suckers

Most roses are made up of the flowering topgrowth and a separate, vigorous root system, onto which the topgrowth has been grafted. Sometimes a shoot fires up from the roots, often with different thorns and leaves. Scrape away the soil to expose the base of the sucker, and tug it off (don't use pruners) or energy will be channeled into this unwanted growth.

Wear gloves to grip sucker and pull out

Deadheading

When a flower starts fading, promptly snip it off. This encourages repeat-flowering roses to develop even more buds, and stops all roses from putting valuable energy into self-propagation by creating seed when it is not necessary. The exception is roses that later have an excellent show of hips—leave the flowers on or you will not get any hips at all.

◄ Cluster-flowered roses
Nip off the central flower, which fades first; later, remove the whole cluster, cutting back to a lower bud.

► Large- or single-flowered roses
Cut back the faded flower to a healthy bud or sideshoot.

Caring for roses in containers

Some roses can easily be grown in containers. To allow the roots to spread, the pot needs to be at least 12–18in (30–45cm) deep for bush roses, or 10–14in (25–35cm) deep for miniature and patio roses. Place a layer of crocks over the drainage holes to stop the soil from washing out, and then fill with loam-based potting mix. Water regularly, especially in hot weather.

Gap of 1in (2.5cm) between soil surface and rim to allow for watering

Pruning roses

PRUNING IS AN EXCELLENT WAY of improving on nature. It prompts vigorous, new, disease-free growth that replaces the tired and the old, creating a pleasing shape and the best possible show of flowers. It also sends shoots in the required direction (usually outward, away from the center). The best time to do it is in late winter, when the roses are dormant.

Pruning tips

In general, prune shrubby roses quite hard in formal gardens to give a neat shape; in informal gardens you can opt for a light trim and a more carefree look. With all roses (including climbers and ramblers), when pruning for the first time, cut back to just two or three buds from the base to encourage lots of new shoots from low down. After that, follow the advice under each entry.

Correctly angled cut ¼in (5mm) above bud

Bruised tissue slow to heal

Cut slopes toward, not away from bud

Too high above bud

The perfect cut
Use clean, sharp pruners, and make an angled cut just above a bud (*left*). Avoid cuts like those above, which may lead to infection and dieback.

Large-flowered bush roses

Prune the main stems quite hard to an outward-pointing bud to create a balanced, shapely framework. Shape is more important for an individual rose than for several planted close together. The harder the pruning, the fewer the stems, but the flowers will be quite large.

Routine pruning
As with all roses, promptly remove any dead, diseased, and damaged wood.

Prune congested or crossing growth to create an open shape with vigorous stems

Remove weak, spindly shoots of less than pencil thickness

Prune strong stems to 8–10in (20–25cm)

Rambling roses

Ramblers can be let loose into treetops, or trained against walls with their stems tied to wires. After flowering, prune out some of the oldest main stems and trim the sideshoots.

Training
Horizontal training ensures a wide spread of flowering shoots at all heights.

Remove one in three of the oldest stems

Prune sideshoots to encourage new flowering growth

Climbers

To encourage climbers to flower low down and high up, train the stems horizontally so that they produce new shoots. Either tie them in if grown against a wall, or wind them up and around a support, such as a tripod.

Cut back flowered and overlong shoots to maintain shape

Shorten some older stems to strong, young replacements

Tripod-training
Wind the stems around the poles from low down, forcing out an even spread of flowering side-shoots along the stems. Use shortish climbers with flexible stems.

Common problems

The key to growing healthy roses is choosing healthy varieties, growing them well in first-rate, well-fed soil, and applying rose fertilizer in spring and after flowering. If problems do arise, tackle them immediately.

▶ **Powdery mildew**
Often caused by poor feeding and air circulation, and dry soil. Cut off affected parts, spray with fungicide, and water.

◀ **Blackspot**
Caused by fungus. Cut off affected parts, spray with fungicide in spring, and repeat as advised over summer.

▶ **Aphids**
Pick them off by hand or wait to see if the birds eat them, which they invariably do; spray as a last resort.

A-Z of Roses

A

ABRAHAM DARBY ('Auscot')

THE MAIN FLUSH OF LARGE, CUPPED FLOWERS, appearing in small clusters, comes in early summer, with many more following later. The blooms are showy and apricot pink, fading with age, and have a rich, fruity scent. ABRAHAM DARBY is well known for its bushy, rounded, shapely look with strong, arching stems and dark green leaves, making it worth a place in a border. Bear in mind its thorns when choosing its position. Prune shoots in late winter by one-half to two-thirds; harder pruning gives fewer stems with larger flowers, lighter pruning more flowering stems with smaller blooms.

PLANT PROFILE

HEIGHT	5ft (1.5m)
SPREAD	5ft (1.5m)
TYPE	Shrub
HARDINESS	Z5–9
FLOWERING	Summer to autumn

'Agnes'

DELIGHTFULLY SCENTED, LIGHT YELLOW, double flowers first appear in early summer, and there is a second, much smaller show in late summer. The wide open blooms are clearly highlighted against the slightly crinkled, dark green, glossy leaves. Vigorous and disease-free, 'Agnes' makes a graceful, bushy spray of twiggy growth, ideal in a mixed border. It is often listed with the Rugosas in rose catalogs. Prune it in late winter, shortening shoots by one-half to two-thirds. Prune harder for fewer stems with larger flowers, and more lightly for more flowering stems with smaller blooms.

PLANT PROFILE	
HEIGHT 6ft (2m)	
SPREAD 4ft (1.2m)	
TYPE Shrub	
HARDINESS Z2–7 H7–1	
FLOWERING Summer	

A | x *alba* 'Alba Maxima' Great white rose, White rose of York

AN EXCELLENT, TOUGH, VIGOROUS, disease-free shrub, this Alba rose has been popular since the 16th century, and is a must for anyone who loves old garden roses. The sweet-scented, creamy white flowers open with a faint pink tinge, and make a gentle show against the gray-green leaves. The plant is rather gaunt and loose (some would say sloppy) in habit, with occasional large thorns. It is particularly good in cottage gardens. To create a large, impressive shrub, remove only diseased, dead, and damaged growth in late winter. If necessary, at the same time, give a minimal pruning to help produce a balanced shape.

PLANT PROFILE

HEIGHT 7ft (2.2m)

SPREAD 5ft (1.5m)

TYPE Old garden rose

HARDINESS Z3–9

FLOWERING Midsummer

'Albéric Barbier'

A

A BIG HIT SINCE IT WAS INTRODUCED over 100 years ago, 'Albéric Barbier' guarantees strong, vigorous growth. The pointed, pale yellow buds open to reveal apple-scented, 3in- (8cm-) wide, creamy white flowers set against the dark green, glossy leaves. After the initial, highly impressive, early-summer display there is a further scattering of flowers. Grow it up pillars and into trees, to cover an eyesore, or on shady sites. Prune in late summer. For the first two years, prune sideshoots by 3in (8cm) to a strong new shoot. Then prune up to one-third of the oldest main stems back to the ground.

PLANT PROFILE	
HEIGHT To 15ft (5m)	
TYPE Rambler	
HARDINESS Z5–9 H9–7	
FLOWERING Summer	

A 'Albertine'

AN INCREDIBLY POPULAR ROSE, 'Albertine' can be grown in various ways. Allowing space for its vigor, try it trained up a wall, against a pergola, or climbing through a tree, or let it mound up in a cottage-garden border, where it will spread to 15ft (5m). The clusters of salmon-red buds open to flowers with a beautiful mix of copper and pink that are richly scented and last for three weeks. In late summer, for the first two years, prune sideshoots by 3in (8cm) to a strong shoot. In following years, prune up to one-third of the oldest main stems back to ground level. Mildew can be a minor problem.

PLANT PROFILE

HEIGHT To 15ft (5m)

TYPE Rambler

HARDINESS Z5–9 H9–5

FLOWERING Midsummer

'Alchymist'

IT MIGHT FLOWER ONLY ONCE, in early summer, but 'Alchymist' (also spelled 'Alchemist') gets high marks from most growers for its impressive show. It has strongly scented, golden yellow to orange flowers with darker centers. Growth is vigorous, the glossy leaves are an attractive bronze, and the stems can be used as a support for a midsummer-flowering clematis. Avoid pruning for the first two years, but train new shoots into a horizontal position. From the third year, prune in the autumn, after flowering, nipping back the main stems if necessary, and shortening sideshoots by two-thirds.

PLANT PROFILE	
HEIGHT	12ft (4m)
TYPE	Climber
HARDINESS	Z4–9
FLOWERING	Early summer

A ALEC'S RED ('Cored')

ONE OF THE BEST small, cherry red bush roses for the front of the border and cut flowers, ALEC'S RED is equally impressive when grown as a standard. Extremely popular (picking up several awards) since it was introduced in 1970, it starts flowering in early summer and continues all through the season. It has exquisite pointed buds and a rich, strong scent, and the leaves are on the verge of dark green. In late winter, remove all unproductive stems, and prune the remaining stems hard to outward-facing buds at 8–10in (20–25cm). For large, showy flowers, prune harder, leaving just two or three buds.

PLANT PROFILE	
HEIGHT	3ft (1m)
SPREAD	24in (60cm)
TYPE	Bush (large-flowered)
HARDINESS	Z5–9 H9–5
FLOWERING	Summer to autumn

ALEXANDER ('Harlex')

AN EXTREMELY VIGOROUS and disease-resistant bush rose, ALEXANDER has a lavish supply of large, showy, vermilion flowers set off by glossy, dark green leaves. It packs plenty of punch in a border, where it is a real eye-catcher, with its flowers held up on long stems. It can also be grown in a row, making a flowery divide or head-high hedge. In late winter, remove all unproductive stems. Prune the remaining stems hard to outward-facing buds, leaving 8–10in (20–25cm) of stem above ground. This helps keep the center of the bush clear. If you want larger blooms, prune to two or three buds.

PLANT PROFILE

HEIGHT	To 6ft (2m)
SPREAD	32in (80cm)
TYPE	Bush (large-flowered)
HARDINESS	Z5–9 H9–5
FLOWERING	Summer to autumn

A | 'Alister Stella Gray'

EXTREMELY RELIABLE AND REPEAT-FLOWERING, this is a
medium-high climber with loose, yolk yellow flowers, 2⅖in
(6cm) wide, which fade to white. The stems are thorn-free, the
scent subtle, and the leaves dark green. Train it up a tree, over
an arch or pergola, or against a wall. The continuous show of
yellow gives a good background for other climbers, including
blue and red varieties of clematis. In the first two years, simply
train new shoots into a horizontal position. After that, prune
in autumn, nipping back the main stems if they outgrow their
space, and shortening sideshoots by two-thirds.

PLANT PROFILE

HEIGHT To 15ft (5m)

TYPE Climber

HARDINESS Z6–9 H9–6

FLOWERING Summer to autumn

'Aloha'

A

CLIMBERS DO NOT HAVE TO SHOOT HIGH into the treetops. This one is short and restrained, ideal for training around pillars or up walls. Everything about it is virtually perfect—the healthy, glossy foliage, fat round buds, and multipetaled flowers with a sweet scent and a hint of orange-pink in the center. After the first main flush of flowers, it is rarely out of bud. For the first two years, train new shoots into a horizontal position, tying them into wires, or spiraling them around a pillar. From the third year, after flowering, prune by trimming the main stems as needed and shortening sideshoots.

PLANT PROFILE

HEIGHT To 10ft (3m)

TYPE Climber

HARDINESS Z5–9 H9–5

FLOWERING Summer to autumn

A

'Alpine Sunset'

THE NAME IS JUST RIGHT because the petals of 'Alpine Sunset'
mix peach, apricot, and yellow. The scented blooms are
surprisingly large, and seem to take so much out of the plant
that there can be a gap after the first flush before more appear.
But 'Alpine Sunset' does repeat-flower, and excels at the front
of a border. With the flowers on short, strong stems, the whole
plant is compact, with glossy, light green leaves. In late winter,
remove all unproductive stems. For large, showy flowers, prune
the remaining stems to two or three buds. Otherwise, prune to
an outward-facing bud 8–10in (20–25cm) from the ground.

PLANT PROFILE

HEIGHT 24in (60cm)

SPREAD 24in (60cm)

TYPE Bush (large-flowered)

HARDINESS Z5–9 H9–5

FLOWERING Summer to autumn

ALTISSIMO ('Delmur')

A RESTRAINED CLIMBER, ALTISSIMO can also be grown, with gentle pruning, as an 8ft- (2.5m-) high shrub. Either way, you get flashy, bright blood red flowers with a faint scent against dark green leaves. Extra flowers follow the first flush, giving a continuous show. Training is vital: unless the new stems on a young plant are trained in a horizontal position, forcing out new branches, all the flowers may appear at the top, out of reach and sight. Pruning is not needed for the first two years. From the third year, after flowering, nip back the main stems if they are too long and shorten sideshoots by two-thirds.

PLANT PROFILE	
HEIGHT 10ft (3m)	
TYPE Climber	
HARDINESS Z5–9	
FLOWERING Summer to autumn	

A | AMBER QUEEN ('Harroony')

WITH A STACK OF AWARDS to its name, AMBER QUEEN is likely to win prizes at most shows, while also brightening up the garden. Short and compact in habit, it can be grown in massed displays or right at the front of a border. The scented flowers have a clean, pure color (nicely set off by the leathery, dark green foliage), and give a constant show all season. Prune in late winter, cutting back the main stems to 10–18in (25–45cm) above ground level, and reducing sideshoots by about one-third of their length.

PLANT PROFILE

HEIGHT	20in (50cm)
SPREAD	24in (60cm)
TYPE	Bush (cluster-flowered)
HARDINESS	Z5–9 H9–5
FLOWERING	Summer to autumn

'American Pillar'

A

THE OPEN FLOWERS ARE A MIX of bright, rich pink around the outside of the petals, with a white eye and yellow central stamens. As its name suggests, grow 'American Pillar' around pillars and into trees. A big favorite in cottage gardens, it is a rampant rose and also makes a beautiful show on a pergola or rustic arch. Prune in late summer. To form the basic framework, prune sideshoots by 3in (8cm) to a strong new shoot for the first two years. In the following years, prune up to one-third of the oldest main stems back to ground level. The glossy, leathery leaves sometimes get a touch of mildew.

PLANT PROFILE

HEIGHT To 15ft (5m)

TYPE Rambler

HARDINESS Z5–9 H9–5

FLOWERING Midsummer

A | ANGELA RIPPON ('Ocaru')

LARGE CLUSTERS OF SALMON PINK FLOWERS, each urn-shaped and about 1½in (4cm) across, are striking against the dark green leaves of ANGELA RIPPON. This twiggy, miniature bush rose is ideal for growing in pots or in substantial gaps between paving. Its prettiness is often best isolated so that it is not lost against the great clamor of taller, summer-flowering plants. Pruning aims to force up plenty of new, vigorous growth: in late winter, remove all growth except for the strongest shoots, and then cut these back by one-third to one-half.

PLANT PROFILE

HEIGHT	18in (45cm)
SPREAD	12in (30cm)
TYPE	Bush (miniature)
HARDINESS	Z5–9 H9–5
FLOWERING	Summer to autumn

ANISLEY DICKSON ('Dickimono')

A GREAT ABUNDANCE OF SMALL FLOWERS, held in clusters, keeps appearing all through the summer. The flowers are neither too lipstick-bright nor too pale, but a reddish pink. Since the supply of fattening buds is so constant, you can take as many as you want for cut flowers. The glossy leaves are dark green. It can be used as a flowering mini-hedge, or as a bush plant for the border. In late winter, cut back the main stems to 10–18in (25–45cm) above the ground, and trim the sideshoots by about one-third of their length.

PLANT PROFILE
HEIGHT 3ft (1m)
SPREAD 30in (75cm)
TYPE Bush (cluster-flowered)
HARDINESS Z5–9 H9–5
FLOWERING Summer to autumn

A

ANNA FORD ('Harpiccolo')

A PERFECT, SCALED-DOWN ROSE for edging, pots, and the front of a border, ANNA FORD has bright, rich orange-red flowers with yellow in the middle. It also flowers all summer, and has bushy growth and dark, glossy green leaves. Since its height of 18in (45cm) is usually borderline between the patio roses and the shorter miniatures, ANNA FORD might be listed in either group in rose catalogs. In late winter, select the strongest shoots and remove the rest. Trim the remaining shoots by one-third to one-half to encourage plenty of new, vigorous, flowering growth.

PLANT PROFILE	
HEIGHT 18in (45cm)	
SPREAD 16in (40cm)	
TYPE Bush (cluster-flowered, miniature)	
HARDINESS Z5–9 H9–5	
FLOWERING Summer to autumn	

ANNA LIVIA ('Kormetter')

WITH BEAUTIFUL SPRAYS OF PINK FLOWERS all summer and a pleasing, uniform shape, this rose produces bushy growth covered by leathery leaves. Though it hardly scores any points for its weak scent, ANNA LIVIA is reliably disease-free and has won an impressive number of awards. It is named after James Joyce's character Anna Livia in his novel *Finnegans Wake*. Use it in pastel plans toward the front of a border where it can be clearly seen. In late winter, cut back the main stems to 10–18in (25–45cm) above the ground, and reduce the sideshoots by about one-third of their length.

PLANT PROFILE

HEIGHT 30in (75cm)

SPREAD 24in (60cm)

TYPE Bush (cluster-flowered)

HARDINESS Z6–9

FLOWERING Summer to autumn

A ANNE HARKNESS ('Harkaramel')

IF YOU NEED A FIRST-RATE ROSE to start opening its flowers when the midsummer old garden roses have faded, this is a very good choice. ANNE HARKNESS bursts into flower in the last part of summer with spectacular flower sprays, making it excellent for a medium-high, mixed rose hedge, and ideal for arrangers. Growth is vigorous, strong, and upright, with healthy foliage. In late winter, cut back the main stems to 10–18in (25–45cm) above ground level, and reduce the sideshoots by about two-thirds of their length.

PLANT PROFILE

HEIGHT 4ft (1.2m)

SPREAD 24in (60cm)

TYPE Bush (cluster-flowered)

HARDINESS Z5–9 H9–5

FLOWERING Late summer to autumn

'Arthur Bell'

SURPRISINGLY WELL SCENTED FOR THIS TYPE OF ROSE, 'Arthur Bell' has many outstanding qualities: it is early flowering, withstands lashing summer downpours, clearly presents its flowers on stiff stems, and has glossy leaves and good disease resistance. It does need to be grown against a dark background, though, because the yellow flowers end up being virtually cream-colored. Prune in late winter, reducing the main stems to 10–18in (25–45cm) high, and cutting back sideshoots by about one-third of their length.

PLANT PROFILE

HEIGHT	3ft (1m)
SPREAD	24in (60cm)
TYPE	Bush (cluster-flowered)
HARDINESS	Z5–9
FLOWERING	Summer to autumn

A | AWAKENING ('Probuzini')

QUITE A STAR, with open, petal-packed flowers of the gentlest pink over summer and a sweet scent, AWAKENING was found growing in Czechoslovakia and introduced to northwest Europe in 1990. If you're looking for an alternative to the pink climber 'New Dawn' (*see page 201*), this is an excellent choice. Growth is not too rampant, making it ideal for arches and medium-high walls. Avoid pruning for the first couple of years, but train shoots horizontally. Once established, prune in the autumn, after flowering, nipping back the main stems if they are too long, and reducing sideshoots by two-thirds.

PLANT PROFILE

HEIGHT 10ft (3m)

TYPE Climber

HARDINESS Z5–9

FLOWERING Summer to autumn

BABY MASQUERADE ('Tanba')

POPULAR FOR OVER 50 YEARS, and for very good reason, the flowers of BABY MASQUERADE change color, starting off bright yellow before becoming flushed with a pinkish red. Keep snipping off the fading blooms to encourage more and more. Growth is on the tall side for a miniature rose, and it forms a bushy plant with leathery leaves. Like other tall miniatures, it can be grown as edging, in pots, or right at the front of a border. In late winter, remove all growth except for the strongest shoots, and prune these back by one-third to one-half to force up plenty of new, vigorous, twiggy shoots.

PLANT PROFILE	
HEIGHT	16in (40cm)
SPREAD	16in (40cm)
TYPE	Bush (miniature)
HARDINESS	Z5–9 H9–5
FLOWERING	Summer to autumn

B | 'Ballerina'

A SUBTLE MIX OF CLEAR, LIGHT PINK COLORING around the edge of each flower and the white color within distinguishes the blooms of 'Ballerina'. The flowers are quite small at 1¼in (3cm) wide, but appear in massed sprays so that you can hardly see the leaves in midsummer when it is in full bloom. The scent is barely noticeable. Further flowers keep appearing all summer on the strong growth. 'Ballerina' can also be grown as a standard. To create a large shrub, remove only diseased, dead, and damaged growth in late winter and give a light trim for shape. If you prune harder, fewer, larger flowers will result.

PLANT PROFILE	
HEIGHT To 5ft (1.5m)	
SPREAD 4ft (1.2m)	
TYPE Shrub	
HARDINESS Z5–9	
FLOWERING Summer to autumn	

banksiae 'Lutea' Yellow banksian rose

A GOOD CHOICE FOR A STURDY TREE, this vigorous rose flowers in mid- to late spring and combines well with a summer-flowering clematis. The profusion of small, double yellow flowers on thornless stems makes a magnificent sight when shoots reach the crown of a tree, but a warm, sheltered site is required. In late summer, for the first two years only, prune sideshoots by 3in (8cm) to a strong new shoot. In the following years, prune up to one-third of the oldest main stems back to ground level.

PLANT PROFILE	
HEIGHT	To 20ft (6m)
TYPE	Rambler
HARDINESS	Z8–9 H9–8
FLOWERING	Mid- to late spring

B | 'Bantry Bay'

A FINE, MODEST CLIMBER FOR A WALL OR PILLAR, 'Bantry Bay'
is always in flower over summer with rich pink blooms. Its
free-branching habit means that it is liberally covered in color,
making it useful as a summer divide or as part of a hedge. It is
remarkably healthy and will not get mildew even if grown
against a wall. All it lacks is a rich, strong scent. Do not prune
for the first two years, but train new shoots horizontally along
their supports or around a pillar. From the third year, prune in
the autumn, after flowering, nipping back the main stems, and
shortening sideshoots by two-thirds.

PLANT PROFILE

HEIGHT 12ft (4m)

TYPE Climber

HARDINESS Z5–9

FLOWERING Summer to autumn

'Baron Girod de l'Ain'

B

A RATHER UNUSUAL ROSE, 'Baron Girod de l'Ain' is a Hybrid Perpetual with strong crimson flowers. Individual petals have a wavy outer edge colored white. Put it at the front of a border where it can be easily seen (it is not too prickly) and you can get a whiff of its sweet scent. A must for lovers of old garden roses, it flowers prolifically over summer and has plenty of vigorous growth. In formal gardens, prune shoots by one-half to two-thirds in late winter. In less formal and cottage gardens, remove only diseased, dead, and damaged growth, and give a light overall pruning for shape.

PLANT PROFILE	
HEIGHT 4ft (1.2m)	
SPREAD 3ft (1m)	
TYPE Old garden rose	
HARDINESS Z5–9	
FLOWERING Summer	

B | 'Belle de Crécy'

BELONGING TO PROBABLY THE OLDEST GROUP OF ROSES, the Gallicas, 'Belle de Crécy' provides everything you could need. There is one powerful burst of richly scented flowers in midsummer, and their color changes from cerise-pink on opening to a softer hue (the color change speeds up in hot weather). Growth is on the lax, arching side, the stems have few thorns, and the leaves are dark green. In late winter, remove diseased, dead, and damaged growth. If needed, prune shoots for a balanced shape—harder pruning results in fewer stems with larger flowers, and lighter pruning the reverse.

PLANT PROFILE

HEIGHT 4ft (1.2m)

SPREAD 3ft (1m)

TYPE Old garden rose

HARDINESS Z3–9 H9–1

FLOWERING Midsummer

'Blairii Number Two'

B

DEEP PINK IN THE CENTER, and pale pink around the outside, 'Blairii Number Two' is a climbing old garden rose, extremely popular for its large, petal-packed, scented flowers. Its one main flowering burst is worth waiting for, and there may be a few sporadic flowers after that. Grow it up pillars, on walls, or over pergolas, but look out for the nasty prickles and mildew. The young leaves are reddish green. In the first two years, train new shoots into a horizontal position. Then start pruning in the autumn, after flowering, cutting back the main stems if necessary and reducing sideshoots by two-thirds.

PLANT PROFILE
HEIGHT 12ft (4m)
TYPE Climber
HARDINESS Z5–9
FLOWERING Midsummer

B 'Blanche Double de Coubert'

MAKING AN EXCELLENT SHRUB ROSE for the border, or an
open summer hedge or divide, 'Blanche Double de Coubert'
has scented white flowers (highlighted against the dark,
leathery foliage) in early summer. They keep appearing all
through the summer, although the soft, papery petals suffer
after heavy rain. It has been extremely popular since being
introduced in France in 1892 and is often listed with Rugosa
roses in catalogs. Prune shoots in late winter by one-half to
two-thirds. Prune lightly for more flowering stems with
smaller blooms, and harder for fewer stems with larger flowers.

PLANT PROFILE

HEIGHT 5ft (1.5m)

SPREAD 4ft (1.2m)

TYPE Shrub

HARDINESS Z3–9 H9–1

FLOWERING Summer to autumn;
hips in late autumn

'Blessings'

B

A TOTALLY RELIABLE front-of-the-border rose, 'Blessings' keeps flowering all summer. The pink flowers (set against dark green leaves) withstand the rain and appear in such numbers that there are always plenty to spare for cutting, though they have minimal scent. They are an extremely useful choice in pastel color schemes or where bolder colors need to be offset by a gentler tone. In late winter, remove all unproductive stems, and prune the remaining ones to outward-facing buds 8–10in (20–25cm) above ground level. For large, showy flowers, prune harder, leaving just two or three buds.

PLANT PROFILE

HEIGHT	3½ft (1.1m)
SPREAD	30in (75cm)
TYPE	Bush (large-flowered)
HARDINESS	Z5–9 H9–5
FLOWERING	Summer to autumn

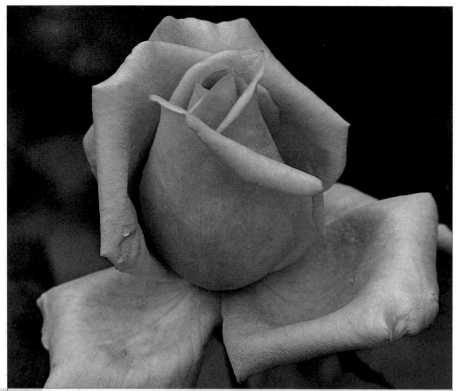

B | BLUE MOON ('Tannacht')

THE BEAUTIFUL FLOWERS OF BLUE MOON are high-pointed when in bud, and good for cutting. The name is misleading because the flowers are not blue but closer to lavender, and they appear on long stems. If grown in dappled shade rather than bright sun, the color will seem slightly darker. Growth is not too vigorous, and the leaves are dark green. In late winter, remove all unproductive stems to ground level, and prune the rest hard to outward-facing buds 8–10in (20–25cm) above the soil. This helps keep the center of the bush clear. For large, showy flowers, prune harder to just two or three buds.

PLANT PROFILE

HEIGHT 3ft (1m)

SPREAD 28in (70cm)

TYPE Bush (large-flowered)

HARDINESS Z6–9

FLOWERING Summer to autumn

'Bobbie James'

B

IF YOU WANT A VIGOROUS, HIGH-POWERED RAMBLER to shoot into a tree, produce masses of clusters of buds, and then erupt in a great display of white flowers (once a summer), this is an excellent choice. Since it was introduced in 1960, it has been a big favorite, not least for its healthy foliage and strong scent. Make sure that you give it plenty of room because this is not a rambler for a small, cramped space. For the first two years after planting, prune sideshoots by 3in (8cm) to a strong, new shoot in late summer. Then prune up to one-third of the oldest stems back to ground level, leaving the new, productive ones.

PLANT PROFILE	
HEIGHT To 30ft (10m)	
TYPE Rambler	
HARDINESS Z5–9	
FLOWERING Early summer	

B | BONICA ('Meidomonac')

A FAIL-SAFE ROSE, BONICA is covered in pink flowers from low down, all the way up to the top of the bush, throughout the summer until the weather turns bad in the autumn. The large sprays of flowers are set against the rich green foliage. It can either be grown as a showstopper at the front of a border, or planted in a row to make a small divide across the garden. Sometimes called a groundcover rose, it makes a shrubby mound with a spread greater than its height. Prune when dormant in winter, removing diseased, dead, and damaged growth. Trim lightly to help produce a balanced shape.

PLANT PROFILE

HEIGHT 34in (85cm)

SPREAD 3½ft (1.1m)

TYPE Shrub

HARDINESS Z4–9 H9–1

FLOWERING Summer to autumn

'Boule de Neige'

B

WORTH ITS PLACE IN A MIXED ROSE HEDGE, 'Boule de Neige' is a Bourbon rose that always makes an excellent show. The 3in- (8cm-) wide, scented flowers appear in clusters all summer, while the leaves are glossy, dark green. The name, which translates as "snowball," describes the rounded white flowers but not the opening buds, which have an attractive red tint. In late winter, prune shoots by one-half to two-thirds. Prune harder for fewer stems with larger flowers, and more lightly for more flowering stems with smaller blooms.

PLANT PROFILE

HEIGHT	5ft (1.5m)
SPREAD	4ft (1.2m)
TYPE	Old garden rose
HARDINESS	Z6–9 H9–6
FLOWERING	Summer to autumn

B | 'Bourbon Queen'

A RICHLY SCENTED PINK, the flowers appear mainly in early summer on stems that can be quite vigorous, almost like those of a climber. If pruned to keep it shrubby, 'Bourbon Queen' has pleasantly wayward growth, making it just right for cottage gardens. The long stems have mid-green leaves. Introduced in 1835, this Bourbon rose will still be a big seller in 2035. To keep growth in check, prune stems in late winter by one-half to two-thirds. If you want fewer stems with larger flowers, prune hard; for more flowering stems with smaller blooms, remove less when pruning.

PLANT PROFILE

HEIGHT To 8ft (2.5m)

SPREAD 5ft (1.5m)

TYPE Old garden rose

HARDINESS Z6–9

FLOWERING Summer

BREATH OF LIFE ('Harquanne')

B

WITH APRICOT FLOWERS THAT LAST WELL when cut, gradually taking on a pink tinge, BREATH OF LIFE is a modest climber. It can be grown up small walls or around pillars, but remember to gently bend down its stiff, upright young stems until they are horizontal so that they put out more flowering shoots low down; otherwise all the flowers will appear high up and out of reach. Leave it unpruned for the first two years, then prune in the autumn, after flowering, nipping back the main stems if necessary and shortening sideshoots by two-thirds.

PLANT PROFILE	
HEIGHT 8ft (2.5m)	
TYPE Climber	
HARDINESS Z5–9 H9–5	
FLOWERING Summer to autumn	

B | BRIGHT SMILE ('Dicdance')

NEAT, BUSHY, AND LOW-GROWING (in fact, so low that some catalogs list it as a patio rose), BRIGHT SMILE offers large, open flowers and tight, slender buds, which keep emerging through the growing season. It is a summery mix of bright yellow, gently scented flowers and glossy, bright green leaves. Small, high-value roses like this are worth including in most gardens, either at the front of a border or to edge paths. Prune in late winter, removing all growth except the strongest shoots. Cut these back by one-third to one-half to force up plenty of new, vigorous growth.

PLANT PROFILE	
HEIGHT	18in (45cm)
SPREAD	18in (45cm)
TYPE	Bush (cluster-flowered, miniature)
HARDINESS	Z5–9 H9–5
FLOWERING	Summer to autumn

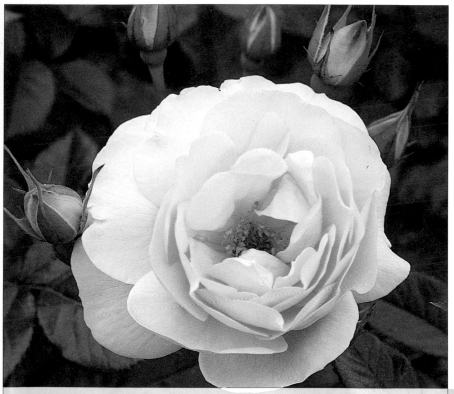

BROADLANDS ('Tanmirson')

B

BROAD IS AN APPROPRIATE DESCRIPTION for this wide-spreading, low-growing, healthy rose, which keeps flowering all summer. The scented flowers are flashy yellow, and the leaves light green. Growth is vigorous, and though it is not so dense and tangled as to keep down and suppress weeds, it will create a flowery background for ponds, adding shade for the frogs and toads. Minimal pruning is required, but if growth is getting too rampant, cut it back to an outward-facing bud in late winter. Shorten sideshoots at the same time if necessary.

PLANT PROFILE	
HEIGHT	20in (50cm)
SPREAD	5ft (1.5m)
TYPE	Groundcover
HARDINESS	Z5–9
FLOWERING	Summer

B | 'Buff Beauty'

AN EXCELLENT, BUSHY SHRUB, 'Buff Beauty' adds plenty of impact when grown against a wall or fence, and it can also be grown as a standard. It has sweet-scented, marmalade or apricot flowers that gently fade, and dark, glossy leaves, adding a muted contrast to the color scheme. The young stems are an attractive reddish brown. The main burst of flowers (in large trusses) is in midsummer, with more following. Prune in late winter to remove diseased, dead, and damaged growth, leaving the old wood intact. If you need to create a more balanced shape, trim the remaining shoots.

PLANT PROFILE

HEIGHT 4ft (1.2m)

SPREAD 4ft (1.2m)

TYPE Shrub

HARDINESS Z6–10 H10–6

FLOWERING Summer

'Camaïeux'

C

THIS EXTRAORDINARY GALLICA ROSE has striped, scented flowers, which appear in one burst in midsummer. They are reddish pink, turning a lavender-lilac purple, splashed or striped with white. It might sound somewhat brash but the effect is surprisingly subtle. Though the plant is on the short side, growth is vigorous. Use it among a collection of old garden roses. To prune, remove diseased, dead, and damaged growth in late winter. Cut back lightly to give a balanced shape with many stems and smaller blooms, or prune harder for fewer stems with larger flowers.

PLANT PROFILE	
HEIGHT	32in (80cm)
SPREAD	32in (80cm)
TYPE	Old garden rose
HARDINESS	Z3–9
FLOWERING	Midsummer

C | *canina* Dog rose

ONE FOR THE WILD OR COTTAGE GARDEN, the dog rose is often seen in wild hedgerows, where its stems make plenty of dense, tangled growth. It is best known for its show of red hips, which are full of vitamin C and are used to make rosehip syrup. The dog rose is not necessarily the best rose for hedges, since it is not particularly showy, but it is of value to wildlife, and its thorny growth should deter most intruders, animal or human. It is hard to prune due to its dense habit; remove only diseased, dead, and damaged growth, and trim overlong shoots to create a balanced shape.

PLANT PROFILE

HEIGHT To 10ft (3m)

SPREAD 6ft (2m)

TYPE Wild

HARDINESS Z5–7

FLOWERING Summer; hips in autumn

'Cantabrigiensis'

C

MAKING ITS FIRST APPEARANCE in Cambridge Botanic Garden in the 1930s, 'Cantabrigiensis' makes vigorous, shrubby growth, with pale yellow flowers opening right at the end of spring for a few weeks. It is a marvelous sight, at its best in cottage or wildflower gardens. It also provides a colorful link between the main burst of spring-flowering plants and those opening at the start of the summer season. Keep pruning to a minimum, removing only diseased, dead, and damaged growth, and trimming unruly shoots in late winter for a balanced shape.

PLANT PROFILE	
HEIGHT 8ft (2.5m)	
SPREAD 8ft (2.5m)	
TYPE Shrub	
HARDINESS Z5–9	
FLOWERING Late spring and early summer; hips in autumn	

C 'Cardinal de Richelieu'

AMONG THE VERY BEST of the old Gallica roses, 'Cardinal de Richelieu' has one superb flush of flowers before midsummer. The blooms are richly colored (dark to royal purple) with a sweet scent, set against dark green leaves. Even the round buds are attractive. There are few thorns, and the overall shape is on the neat and tidy side. Give it a prominent place where you can smell the flowers. To create an impressive shrub, remove only diseased, dead, and damaged growth, and leave the old wood intact. In late winter trim long shoots to give a balanced shape. Harder pruning gives fewer stems with larger flowers.

PLANT PROFILE	
HEIGHT 3ft (1m)	
SPREAD 4ft (1.2m)	
TYPE Old garden rose	
HARDINESS Z3–9 H9–1	
FLOWERING Summer	

CASINO ('Macca')

C

A FIRST-RATE CLIMBER, with soft yellow, gently scented
flowers that emerge from pointed buds and slowly fade. At
10ft (3m) high, it does not get out of hand, and is an excellent
choice for a trellis, pergola, or small wall. The dark green
leaves are slightly sparse. It dislikes cold, exposed areas, and is
therefore best in a sunny, protected site. As new shoots develop
over the first two years, train them horizontally to produce
flowering sideshoots. Once the shape of the plant is
established, prune in the autumn after flowering, trimming the
main stems as needed, and reducing sideshoots by two-thirds.

PLANT PROFILE	
HEIGHT 10ft (3m)	
TYPE Climber	
HARDINESS Z5–9 H9–5	
FLOWERING Summer to autumn	

C | 'Cécile Brünner'

SMALL, TWIGGY, AND PRETTY are the best words to describe this China rose. Large clusters of petite, beautiful flowers open from pointed, shapely buds. The growth is twiggy, and the show of dark green leaves is on the sparse side. The overall shape has a light, neat touch, making it excellent for small courtyards or tubs where nothing too bulky is required. It is a popular plant for the almost-constant show of flowers through the growing season. Prune it in late winter, cutting shoots by one-half to two-thirds. Pruning by two-thirds will give fewer stems with larger flowers.

PLANT PROFILE

HEIGHT	30in (75cm)
SPREAD	24in (60cm)
TYPE	Old garden rose
HARDINESS	Z5–9 H9–1
FLOWERING	Summer to autumn

'Céleste'

C

'CÉLESTE' IS HIGHLY VALUED for its attractive, dark pink buds, which open to reveal shell pink, scented flowers with yellow stamens. The lightness of tone blends well with the gray-green leaves. It is sometimes listed as 'Celestial' in catalogs, where it usually appears with the Alba roses. It tolerates less-than-ideal growing conditions and can be grown as a hedge. To maintain it as a large shrub, remove only diseased, dead, and damaged growth. A minimal late winter pruning gives a balanced shape. For fewer but larger flowers, prune harder, otherwise it will produce more stems with smaller blooms.

PLANT PROFILE	
HEIGHT 5ft (1.5m)	
SPREAD 4ft (1.2m)	
TYPE Old garden rose	
HARDINESS Z3–9 H9–1	
FLOWERING Midsummer	

C | *x centifolia* 'Cristata' Crested moss rose

SOME ROSES ARE GROWN more for their neat, tidy growth, and
some for their excellent flowers; this Moss rose is definitely
one of the latter. The shape is lax and open, and some
gardeners stake the stems to stop them from bending down,
though that is not a problem in easy-going cottage gardens.
The branching, arching stems are covered in rose pink flowers,
and the opening buds are equally stunning. To create and
maintain the naturally striking, lax bush shape, remove only
diseased, dead, and damaged growth in winter, and leave the
old wood intact. Little other pruning is required.

PLANT PROFILE

HEIGHT 5ft (1.5m)

SPREAD 4ft (1.2m)

TYPE Old garden rose

HARDINESS Z4–9 H9–1

FLOWERING Summer

x *centifolia* 'Muscosa' Common moss rose

INTERESTING MOSSY GROWTH on the lax, prickly stems and just below the attractive, deep pink flowers makes *Rosa x centifolia* 'Muscosa' appealing to plant collectors, among others. Like the similar *R. x centifolia* 'Cristata' (*see opposite page*), it is generally listed in rose catalogs with the group called Moss roses, which were a big hit in Victorian times. Minimal pruning is needed: remove only diseased, dead, and damaged growth to obtain a large, impressive shrub. If you need to trim shoots for a balanced shape, do this in late winter.

PLANT PROFILE	
HEIGHT	5ft (1.5m)
SPREAD	4ft (1.2m)
TYPE	Old garden rose
HARDINESS	Z4–9 H9–1
FLOWERING	Summer

C

'Cerise Bouquet'

A MASSIVE SHRUB ROSE, 'Cerise Bouquet' has enormous presence in the border or as a feature in its own bed in a large lawn. It can also be used in a hedge of mixed roses. Growth is strong and arching, the leaves are gray-green, and the clusters of 2⅓in- (6cm-) wide flowers are lipstick red. There is sometimes a second crop of flowers toward the end of summer. Prune in late winter. If you would like fewer, larger flowers, prune hard. Otherwise, prune lightly, removing diseased, dead, and damaged growth, and leaving the old wood intact; select overlong shoots to trim for a balanced shape.

PLANT PROFILE	
HEIGHT To 11ft (3.5m)	
SPREAD To 11ft (3.5m)	
TYPE Shrub	
HARDINESS Z5–9	
FLOWERING Summer	

'Charles de Mills'

ONE OF THE BEST-LOVED GALLICA ROSES, 'Charles de Mills' is popular for two reasons: it has large, lightly scented, petal-packed flowers, about 4in (10cm) wide, which have an incredibly flat surface; and the color is rich, dark red with hints of lilac and purple. Growth is vigorous, sometimes even arching, and the lack of prickles makes it good for the front of a border. For a large shrub, remove only diseased, dead, and damaged growth. An additional light, late-winter pruning gives a balanced shape and encourages more stems with smaller blooms. Harder pruning gives fewer stems with larger flowers.

PLANT PROFILE

HEIGHT	4ft (1.2m)
SPREAD	4ft (1.2m)
TYPE	Old garden rose
HARDINESS	Z3–9 H9–1
FLOWERING	Midsummer

C

'Chinatown'

THE WELL-SCENTED, YELLOW FLOWERS have a slight pink tinge, and they cover the stems through most of the summer, making a vigorous show and even withstanding bad weather. The attractive background leaf color is glossy, dark green. Tough and reliable, 'Chinatown' can be used to keep borders alive and colorful, or be incorporated as part of a medium-high mixed hedge. It is a top choice that will not let you down. In late winter, cut back the main stems to 10–18in (25–45cm) above ground level, and reduce sideshoots by about two-thirds of their length.

PLANT PROFILE

HEIGHT 4ft (1.2m)

SPREAD 3ft (1m)

TYPE Bush (cluster-flowered)

HARDINESS Z5–9

FLOWERING Summer to autumn

CIDER CUP ('Dicladida')

ONE OF THE BEST of the more recent patio roses, CIDER CUP has everything you could want except a strong, rich scent. With a small, neat, bushy shape, attractive, high-pointed buds, and a long show of attractive, marmalade-yellow flowers (also good for cutting), it withstands summer rain and still looks good. It is equally effective in pots or when used as an edging plant, or in semicircles in front of a garden statue. Prune to encourage plenty of new, vigorous growth. In late winter, remove all growth apart from the strongest shoots, and then cut them back by one-third to one-half.

PLANT PROFILE	
HEIGHT	18in (45cm)
SPREAD	18in (45cm)
TYPE	Bush (cluster-flowered, patio)
HARDINESS	Z5–9
FLOWERING	Summer

C

CITY OF LONDON ('Harukfore')

THE BEAUTIFULLY SHAPED FLOWERS, soft pink and highly scented, gradually fade in color, and make a gentle addition to pastel borders. Growth is vigorous, clusters of small flowers keep appearing, and the background leaf color is healthy, glossy green. CITY OF LONDON has been deservedly popular since its introduction in 1988. For a reasonably compact bush, in late winter, cut back the main stems to 10–18in (25–45cm) above the ground, and reduce sideshoots by about one-third. If you do not follow the pruning regimen, CITY OF LONDON grows much taller, reaching 5ft (1.5m) or possibly even higher.

PLANT PROFILE

HEIGHT 32in (80cm)

SPREAD 30in (75cm)

TYPE Bush (cluster-flowered)

HARDINESS Z5–9

FLOWERING Summer to autumn

'Climbing Etoile de Hollande'

C

A WONDERFUL CLIMBER, this has lax, arching stems and enormous, richly scented flowers. The large buds start opening in early summer, when it has its main burst of blooms. The crimson flowers have a lovely, sweet scent and, being 5in (13cm) wide, tend to hang down, especially after heavy rain, which adds to the sense of opulence. After the first flush of flowers, more will appear. Avoid pruning for the first two years, but train new shoots into a horizontal position. In the following years, prune in the autumn, nipping back the main stems as needed and shortening sideshoots by two-thirds.

PLANT PROFILE	
HEIGHT	20ft (6m)
TYPE	Climber
HARDINESS	Z6–9
FLOWERING	Summer

C | 'Climbing Lady Hillingdon'

WHILE IT PERFORMS WELL in poor conditions, 'Climbing Lady Hillingdon' is invariably best grown against a hot, sunny wall, where its arching stems produce 3in (8cm) wide flowers that are open and apricot-yellow, with a strong, sweet scent. The new stems are a beautiful red, though it can take a few years for the basic framework to start sending them out. A main burst of flowers in early summer is followed by more. Avoid pruning for the first two years, training new shoots into a horizontal position. Then prune after flowering, cutting back the main stems if necessary and sideshoots by two-thirds.

PLANT PROFILE

HEIGHT To 15ft (5m)

TYPE Climber

HARDINESS Z6–9

FLOWERING Summer to autumn

'Climbing Mrs Sam McGredy'

C

THIS HIGHLY REGARDED CLIMBING VERSION of a large-flowered bush has copper-orange flowers, which sets it apart from the mass of red, pink, and white climbers. The leaves have a bronze tint, the buds are reddish brown, and the flowers are initially high-pointed before they open and flatten out. The display keeps going reliably until autumn. In the first two years, simply train new shoots into a horizontal position to encourage plenty of flowering sideshoots. In the following years, prune in the autumn, after flowering, nipping back the main stems as needed and shortening sideshoots by two-thirds.

PLANT PROFILE	
HEIGHT 15ft (5m)	
TYPE Climber	
HARDINESS Z5–9	
FLOWERING Summer to autumn	

'Compassion'

A HIGH-QUALITY CLIMBER, 'Compassion' has picked up many awards since it was introduced in 1973 because it has all the key ingredients of a successful rose. It has superb scent, beautiful colors, with a touch of apricot to add to the soft pink, and a constant supply of shapely flowers all summer. Modestly rampant, it is ideal for a small wall or pillar, with a covering of glossy leaves. It exudes good health. Avoid pruning for the first two years, but train new shoots into a horizontal position. Once established, prune in the autumn, nipping back the main stems and shortening sideshoots by two-thirds.

PLANT PROFILE

HEIGHT 10ft (3m)

TYPE Climber

HARDINESS Z5–9 H9–5

FLOWERING Summer to autumn

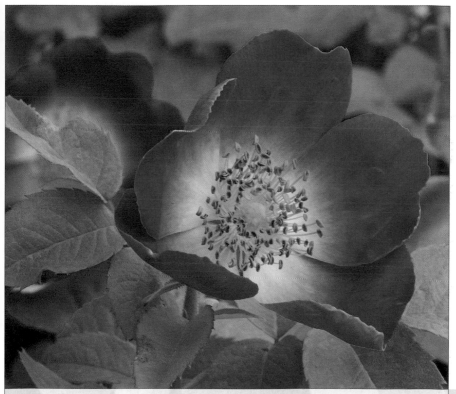

'Complicata'

C

A SUPERB, BUSHY GALLICA ROSE, 'Complicata' has very large, 4in- (10cm-) wide flowers with a gentle scent. What makes them so eye-catching is the white base of the petals and the yellow stamens. Tough and robust, it can be grown as an early summer–flowering hedge or in a garden of old roses, but allow space for its arching stems. To create a large shrub, remove diseased, dead, and damaged growth in late winter, and leave the old wood. Give a minimal trim for a balanced shape and plenty of stems with smaller blooms. If you prune harder, it will produce fewer stems with larger flowers.

PLANT PROFILE	
HEIGHT	7ft (2.2m)
SPREAD	8ft (2.5m)
TYPE	Old garden rose
HARDINESS	Z4–9 H9–1
FLOWERING	Midsummer

C | CONGRATULATIONS ('Korlift')

WITH ITS POINTED BUDS, plenty of flowers (good for cutting) all summer, and dark green leaves, CONGRATULATIONS is a useful addition to a mixed border. It is nearly twice as tall as it is wide, which calls for careful planning when positioning it. An alternative is to plant it in rows to make a summer hedge or divide; being quite narrow, it does not take up too much room. When pruning, you are aiming for an open-centered bush. In late winter, remove all unproductive stems, and prune hard to outward-facing buds 8–10in (20–25cm) above ground level. For larger flowers, prune harder, to two or three buds.

PLANT PROFILE

HEIGHT	5ft (1.5m)
SPREAD	3ft (1m)
TYPE	Bush (large-flowered)
HARDINESS	Z5–9
FLOWERING	Summer to autumn

'Conrad Ferdinand Meyer'

C

A SUPERB ROSE for the back of the border, where its arching, thorny stems bear large, 4in- (10cm-) wide, wonderfully scented flowers. The gray-green leaves are also large. There are usually two flowering bursts, one in early summer and one in early autumn, with the second being better than the first. Growth is vigorous. To create a large shrub, remove only diseased, dead, and damaged growth, and leave the old wood. A light pruning in late winter also helps to give a balanced shape and more flowering stems with smaller blooms. Harder pruning gives fewer stems with larger flowers.

PLANT PROFILE	
HEIGHT 8ft (2.5m)	
SPREAD 6ft (2m)	
TYPE Shrub	
HARDINESS Z4–9 H9–1	
FLOWERING Summer and autumn	

C | CONSERVATION ('Cocdimple')

INTRODUCED TO MARK THE 50TH BIRTHDAY of the World Wildlife Fund, CONSERVATION is a short, compact, bushy, mounding plant that flowers all through the summer. The apricot-pink blooms are nicely set off by the glossy leaves. A high-performance patio rose, it should be highlighted in a pot or grown in gaps where stones have been removed in a large terrace. Prune to keep a good supply of new, vigorous, twiggy growth. In late winter, remove all but the strongest shoots, and then cut them back by one-third to one-half.

PLANT PROFILE

HEIGHT	18in (45cm)
SPREAD	18in (45cm)
TYPE	Bush (cluster-flowered, patio)
HARDINESS	Z5–9
FLOWERING	Summer to autumn

CONSTANCE SPRY ('Austance')

A DUAL-PURPOSE ROSE, CONSTANCE SPRY can be grown as a rampant shrub at the back of a border, or as a moderate climber against a wall, where it will hit 10ft (3m) or more (some catalogs actually list it as a climber). The 5in- (13cm-) wide flowers have a strong scent, and are borne on thorny stems. Although they appear only once, they make a spectacular show. The foliage hangs on over winter, and often needs spraying against mildew in summer. When pruning, remove diseased, dead, and damaged growth, and leave the old wood intact. Cut back lightly to promote a balanced shape.

C

PLANT PROFILE

HEIGHT 6ft (2m) as a shrub; 10ft (3m) as a climber

SPREAD 5ft (1.5m) as a shrub

TYPE Shrub and climber

HARDINESS Z4–9 H9–1

FLOWERING Midsummer

C | 'Cornelia'

IT IS RARE TO GROW A ROSE for its autumn show of flowers, but the best sprays of 'Cornelia', bigger and more richly colored, open just after the end of summer. The first blooms open in early summer and are apricot, fading to pink, against dark green leaves. Its substantial size means it makes an effective hedge, especially where it catches the autumn sun on the copper-red buds. Little pruning is needed: remove only diseased, dead, and damaged growth, and trim overlong shoots in late winter. This minimal regimen encourages many small blooms; harder pruning will result in larger flowers.

PLANT PROFILE

HEIGHT	5ft (1.5m)
SPREAD	5ft (1.5m)
TYPE	Shrub
HARDINESS	Z6–9
FLOWERING	Summer to autumn

'Crimson Glory'

AN EXQUISITE SMALL, CRIMSON ROSE, this has beautifully shaped, velvety flowers with a fabulous scent. They give a long display all through the growing season on bushy growth with dark green leaves. The leaves are prone to mildew and the stems are prickly, but that is no reason to be put off. If you have a gap at the front of a border, or want roses for a corsage, grow it. For a healthy, open-centered bush, remove all unproductive stems in late winter, and prune the remaining ones to outward-facing buds 8–10in (20–25cm) above ground level. For large, showy flowers, prune to just two or three buds.

PLANT PROFILE

HEIGHT	24in (60cm)
SPREAD	24in (60cm)
TYPE	Bush (large-flowered)
HARDINESS	Z5–9
FLOWERING	Summer to autumn

C | 'Crimson Shower'

MOST RAMBLERS TEND TO FLOWER only once in midsummer, but 'Crimson Shower' has a surprisingly long flowering period, starting soon after midsummer and continuing until the beginning of autumn. Train the stems into trees or around pillars or pergolas, where the bright red flowers add plenty of color. For the first two years, prune sideshoots by 3in (8cm) to a strong, new shoot. In the following years, prune at most one-third of the oldest main stems back to ground level. It can also be grown as a very effective weeping standard.

PLANT PROFILE	
HEIGHT 15ft (5m)	
TYPE Rambler	
HARDINESS Z5–9	
FLOWERING Summer to autumn	

X *damascena* var. *semperflorens* Autumn Damask rose

D

ALSO KNOWN AS THE FOUR SEASONS ROSE, this Damask rose has a highly impressive ability to keep flowering from early summer (its main burst) to midautumn (more in sporadic bursts). Unusually, the leaves are light green, and the attractive, scented flowers, which are quite large at nearly 4in (10cm) wide on the arching stems, are clear rose pink. In late winter, prune by one-half to two-thirds. Prune harder for fewer stems with larger flowers, and more lightly for more stems with smaller blooms.

PLANT PROFILE

HEIGHT 5ft (1.5m)

SPREAD 4ft (1.2m)

TYPE Old garden rose

HARDINESS Z4–9

FLOWERING Early summer to midautumn

D | 'Danse du Feu'

A GOOD CLIMBER FOR A COLD, SHADY WALL, 'Danse du Feu'
is at its most attractive when in bud with many flowers half-
open. The blooms have a neat, tight shape and strong color.
As the petals open and lengthen, the color starts to fade to
orange-red, but the repeat-flowering does provide good color
against white walls. Avoid pruning for the first two years, but
train new shoots horizontally to produce flowering sideshoots.
From the third year, prune in the autumn, after flowering,
nipping back the main stems if necessary and shortening
sideshoots by two-thirds.

PLANT PROFILE	
HEIGHT 8ft (2.5m)	
TYPE Climber	
HARDINESS Z5–9 H9–5	
FLOWERING Summer to autumn	

DAWN CHORUS ('Dicquasar')

D

CLASSIC, HIGH-POINTED BUDS open to marmalade orange flowers with a hint of yellow. The very lightly scented flowers are quite prolific, appearing through summer into the start of autumn. DAWN CHORUS holds its own in hot color schemes, and can be used with the likes of subtropical cannas. It can also be grown in a more traditional way, as a standard. In late winter, remove all unproductive stems, and prune hard to outward-facing buds 8–10in (20–25cm) above the ground. This helps deter crisscrossing shoots in the center. For large, showy flowers, prune harder, leaving just two or three buds.

PLANT PROFILE	
HEIGHT 3ft (1m)	
SPREAD 30in (75cm)	
TYPE Bush (large-flowered)	
HARDINESS Z6–9	
FLOWERING Summer to autumn	

D | 'Deep Secret'

ONE OF THE VERY BEST large-flowered bush roses, 'Deep Secret' has exquisitely shapely buds and flowers, a deep, rich red color (even darker in the case of the buds), a sweet scent, glossy green leaves, and bushy growth. It is worth including in any display of roses, makes a very classy standard, and is excellent for cut flowers. Remove unproductive stems in late winter, and prune hard to outward-facing buds 8–10in (20–25cm) from the soil. For large, showy flowers, prune harder, leaving just two or three buds. Cutting to outward-facing buds keeps the center of the bush clear.

PLANT PROFILE

HEIGHT 3ft (1m)

SPREAD 30in (75cm)

TYPE Bush (large-flowered)

HARDINESS Z5–9

FLOWERING Summer to autumn

'Desprez à Fleurs Jaunes'

D

EXCELLENT IN COTTAGE GARDENS, 'Desprez à Fleurs Jaunes' has lax, arching stems and, in early summer, the tight pinkish white buds open to reveal flat-surfaced flowers. They are white from a distance, but up close the color is more creamy white with a gentle tinge of pink and yellow toward the petal edges. The scent is of tangy, freshly cut apples. No pruning is needed for the first two years, but train new shoots horizontally. Then prune in the autumn, after flowering, trimming the main stems if they are too long, and sideshoots by two-thirds.

PLANT PROFILE	
HEIGHT	15ft (5m)
TYPE	Climber
HARDINESS	Z6–9
FLOWERING	Summer

D | 'Doris Tysterman'

OFTEN USED IN BOLD, BRIGHT COLOR SCHEMES, 'Doris Tysterman' has a long summer show of orange-red flowers with darker hues at the edge of the petals. The growth stands smartly upright, holding up the flowers well against the glossy, dark green leaves. It is sometimes prone to mildew. In late winter, remove any unproductive stems, and prune the remainder hard to outward-facing buds at 8–10in (20–25cm) along the stem. This helps remove crisscrossing shoots in the center. For large, showy flowers, prune harder, leaving just two or three buds.

PLANT PROFILE	
HEIGHT 4ft (1.2m)	
SPREAD 30in (75cm)	
TYPE Bush (large-flowered)	
HARDINESS Z5–9 H9–5	
FLOWERING Summer to autumn	

'Dorothy Perkins'

FLOWERING AFTER MOST RAMBLERS ARE FINISHED, in the
second half of summer, 'Dorothy Perkins' is a valuable addition
to the garden, although it does suffer from mildew. It provides
a lavish show of plump, rose pink flowers with quilled petals
against a background of dark green leaves. Either send the
stems up and around a pillar or pergola or into a tree, or grow
them against a wall. In late summer, for the first two years,
prune sideshoots by 3in (8cm) to a strong, new shoot. In
subsequent years, prune up to one-third of the oldest main
stems back to ground level.

PLANT PROFILE

HEIGHT 10ft (3m)

TYPE Rambler

HARDINESS Z5–9

FLOWERING Late summer

D | 'Dortmund'

A PROLIFIC CLIMBER that never gets out of hand, 'Dortmund' immediately stands out with its five-petaled red flowers with a white eye and yellow-orange stamens in the center. It makes an excellent choice for pergolas and pillars, mainly because of its healthy, glossy green foliage and long show of flowers. All it lacks is scent. Avoid pruning for the first two years, simply training new shoots into a horizontal position to produce flowering sideshoots. From the third year, prune in the autumn, after flowering, trimming back the main stems if they outgrow the space and reducing sideshoots by two-thirds.

PLANT PROFILE

HEIGHT 10ft (3m)

TYPE Climber

HARDINESS Z5–9 H9–5

FLOWERING Summer to autumn

'Du Maître d'Ecole'

D

A SUPERB OLD GALLICA ROSE, dating from 1840, 'Du Maître d'Ecole' is grown for its large, 4in- (10cm-) wide, heavy flowers, which are even larger on rich soils. The color begins rose pink, then gradually changes to lilac-pink with a green dot in the center. The flowers are well spaced on upright, almost thorn-free growth with dark green leaves. Some catalogs call this rose 'De la Maître d'Ecole'. To prune, remove only diseased, dead, and damaged growth, and leave the old wood. A minimal late-winter pruning also gives a balanced shape, with harder pruning producing fewer stems with larger flowers.

PLANT PROFILE	
HEIGHT 4ft (1.2m)	
SPREAD 4ft (1.2m)	
TYPE Old garden rose	
HARDINESS Z4–9	
FLOWERING Midsummer	

D | DUBLIN BAY ('Macdub')

AN EXCELLENT RED CLIMBER, DUBLIN BAY has everything you could want in a rose except a satisfying, rich scent. The buds and flowers are shapely (because they belong to the large-flowered group of roses), the color is strong, vivid red, the clusters of blooms give a constant display, and the healthy, glossy foliage completes the package. Avoid pruning for the first two years, but train new shoots into a horizontal position. Then prune in the autumn, nipping back the main stems if they are too long, and cutting back sideshoots by two-thirds. With harder pruning it can also form a shrub.

PLANT PROFILE	
HEIGHT 7ft (2.2m)	
TYPE Climber	
HARDINESS Z5–9 H9–5	
FLOWERING Summer to autumn	

'Duc de Guiche'

ONE OF THE BEST GALLICAS, this should be in every collection of old garden roses. The buds appear in clusters, the 4in- (10cm-) wide flowers are richly colored with a hint of lilac and a tiny green eye in the center, the scent is deep, and the dense growth is gently arching and sprawling. It flowers only once in midsummer, but the display is worth waiting for. Remove diseased, dead, and damaged growth for an impressive shrub, and leave the old wood intact. A minimal late-winter pruning also helps produce a balanced shape. If you prune harder, fewer stems with larger flowers will be produced.

PLANT PROFILE

HEIGHT	4ft (1.2m)
SPREAD	4ft (1.2m)
TYPE	Old garden rose
HARDINESS	Z3–9
FLOWERING	Summer

D | 'Dupontii' Snowbush rose

AT 7FT (2.2M) HIGH, 'Dupontii' makes a large, shrubby plant that can be grown against a wall, as a border background, or in rows to create a substantial hedge. In fact, the closer you can get to smell the flowers, the better, because they have the fruity aroma of bubblegum and bananas. The nearly thornless stems tend to arch, and have gray-green leaves. The flowers are followed by orange autumn hips. Remove diseased, dead, and damaged growth and, in late winter, prune lightly to produce a balanced shape and plenty of stems with small blooms. If you prune harder, the rose will produce fewer but larger flowers.

PLANT PROFILE

HEIGHT 7ft (2.2m)

SPREAD 7ft (2.2m)

TYPE Shrub

HARDINESS Z4–9 H9–1

FLOWERING Midsummer; hips in autumn

'Dutch Gold'

D

THE SCENTED FLOWERS OF 'DUTCH GOLD' are large (good for cutting) and can reach 6in (15cm) wide; the bright yellow color does not fade, and the flowers withstand bad weather and rain. It is well covered in large, glossy, dark green leaves and is a good choice for the front of a border. It might be small, but it is a vigorous bush rose. Remove all unproductive stems in late winter, and prune hard to outward-facing buds at 8–10in (20–25cm). For large, showy flowers, prune harder, leaving just two or three buds.

PLANT PROFILE	
HEIGHT	3½ft (1.1m)
SPREAD	30in (75cm)
TYPE	Bush (large-flowered)
HARDINESS	Z5–9
FLOWERING	Summer to autumn

E | EGLANTYNE ('Ausmak')

THE PALE PINK FLOWERS have the rich scent of an old garden rose and keep flowering for a long period over summer. The growth is modest, twiggy, and bushy, with attractive green leaves, and is ideally suited to pastel gardens with mixed planting. EGLANTYNE also makes a graceful show when set in rows to edge a path. The cut flowers last for a long time in water. Prune shoots by one-half to two-thirds in late winter. The harder you prune, the fewer the resulting stems and the larger the flowers.

PLANT PROFILE

HEIGHT 3½ft (1.1m)

SPREAD 3ft (1m)

TYPE Shrub

HARDINESS Z4–9

FLOWERING Summer

ELINA ('Dicjana')

E

STILL KNOWN TO SOME AS 'PEAUDOUCE', this rose has a handful of top awards. It is a beauty in the garden and worth growing because of its large flowers (virtually scentless) up to 6in (15cm) wide, which withstand the summer rain. They are nicely highlighted against the disease-resistant, glossy, dark green leaves. Even the fattening buds look stylish. Prune in late winter, removing all unproductive stems, and cutting to outward-facing buds, leaving 8–10in (20–25cm) of stem above ground. This helps discourage crossing shoots in the center. For larger, more showy flowers, prune to two or three buds.

PLANT PROFILE	
HEIGHT	3½ft (1.1m)
SPREAD	30in (75cm)
TYPE	Bush (large-flowered)
HARDINESS	Z4–11 H12–1
FLOWERING	Summer to autumn

E | 'Elizabeth Harkness'

EXPERTS WAX LYRICAL ABOUT THIS ROSE, calling it "refined."
The flowers are creamy white, tinged with rose pink, and are
attractively shaped, with the first opening in early summer and
the display continuing until autumn, against dark green leaves.
Lean in close to get a whiff of the sweet scent. It makes a
good choice for borders and rose gardens, as well as cut-flower
arrangements. When pruning, you are aiming for an open-
centered bush. In late winter, remove all unproductive stems,
and cut the rest to outward-facing buds at 8–10in (20–25cm).
For large, showy flowers, prune to two or three buds.

PLANT PROFILE

HEIGHT 32in (80cm)

SPREAD 24in (60cm)

TYPE Bush (large-flowered)

HARDINESS Z5–9 H9–5

FLOWERING Summer to autumn

'Emily Gray'

IF YOU WANT BUFF-YELLOW or yellowish marmalade flowers, this is the rambler to choose. The scented flowers are not as prolific as on some ramblers but you will still have a very good display, and the stems put on plenty of growth. Most of the leaves hang on all year, especially in mild regions, and when the new spring foliage appears, it turns from attractive copper-red to glossy dark green. In late summer, for the first couple of years, prune sideshoots by 3in (8cm) to a strong, new shoot. In the following years, prune at most one-third of the oldest main stems back to ground level.

PLANT PROFILE

HEIGHT To 15ft (5m)

TYPE Rambler

HARDINESS Z5–9 H9–5

FLOWERING Midsummer

E

'Empereur du Maroc'

RICHLY, EXQUISITELY SCENTED FLOWERS have 40 or so petals with a deep, dark red color, making it one of the darkest of its kind. This high-quality 19th-century Hybrid Perpetual rose is free-flowering over summer, more than making up for its slight tendency to mildew, its prickles, and the fact that it needs plenty of manure to fuel its flowers. In formal gardens, prune shoots by one-half to two-thirds in late winter. In less formal and cottage gardens, remove only diseased, dead, and damaged growth, and give a light overall pruning for shape.

PLANT PROFILE
HEIGHT 4ft (1.2m)
SPREAD 3ft (1m)
TYPE Old garden rose
HARDINESS Z5–9 H9–5
FLOWERING Summer

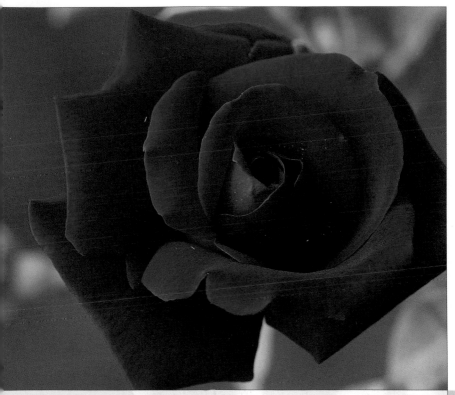

'Ena Harkness'

E

A BIG HIT IN THE 1950s, when gardeners could not get enough of its strong-colored, scented flowers, 'Ena Harkness' was a firm favorite at the front of borders, especially for end-of-season color. There followed a backlash when other roses became more popular thanks to their fuller covering of leaves and stronger flower stalks, but it remains a very good rose. The related 'Climbing Ena Harkness' grows to 15ft (5m). Remove all unproductive stems in late winter, and prune the remainder hard to outward-facing buds at 8–10in (20–25cm). For large, showy flowers, prune harder, leaving just two or three buds.

PLANT PROFILE	
HEIGHT	30in (75cm)
SPREAD	24in (60cm)
TYPE	Bush (large-flowered)
HARDINESS	Z5–9
FLOWERING	Summer to autumn

E

ENGLISH GARDEN ('Ausbuff')

MIXING OLD GARDEN ROSE–TYPE FLOWERS and a modern tendency to repeat-flower, ENGLISH GARDEN (introduced in 1986) has slightly scented flowers, apricot to buff yellow in the center, turning paler toward the edge of the petals. It is good at extending pastel color schemes. ENGLISH GARDEN is taller than it is wide, and is a good candidate for sandwiching in gaps in a border or rose bed. In late winter, prune stems by one-half to two-thirds. Harder pruning will result in fewer stems with larger flowers, and lighter pruning more flowering stems with smaller blooms.

PLANT PROFILE

HEIGHT 3ft (1m)

SPREAD 30in (75cm)

TYPE Shrub

HARDINESS Z5–9

FLOWERING Summer to autumn

'English Miss'

THE NICELY SCENTED FLOWERS have the soft, pale color of a pinkish face and are set against a mass of leathery, dark green leaves. Look closely and you will see that the blooms, which appear all summer long, held in clusters, are packed with up to 60 petals. This is a quiet and gentle beauty with a highly appropriate name. Its small, compact shape makes it a good choice for the front of a bedding plan or border. In late winter, cut back main stems to 10–18in (25–45cm), and trim the sideshoots by about one-third.

PLANT PROFILE	
HEIGHT 3ft (1m)	
SPREAD 24in (60cm)	
TYPE Bush (cluster-flowered)	
HARDINESS Z5–9	
FLOWERING Summer to autumn	

E | 'Ernest H. Morse'

A LOW-GROWING, BRIGHT RED BUSH ROSE, 'Ernest H. Morse' keeps flowering over summer, with shapely, high-pointed buds. On opening, the flowers are nicely scented and 5in (13cm) wide, withstanding rain well, while the leaves are glossy, dark green, and disease-resistant, though they are sometimes susceptible to mildew. Prune in late winter, removing all unproductive stems. Cut back the remainder to outward-facing buds at about 8–10in (20–25cm). This helps prevent the center of the bush from becoming congested with crisscrossing shoots. For large, showy flowers, prune to two or three buds.

PLANT PROFILE

HEIGHT	30in (75cm)
SPREAD	24in (60cm)
TYPE	Bush (large-flowered)
HARDINESS	Z5–9
FLOWERING	Summer to autumn

EVELYN ('Aussaucer')

E

INTRODUCED IN 1991, EVELYN mixes the best of old-rose charm and scent (and the scent is wonderfully fruity) with an ability to repeat-flower. The large flowers begin with just a faint hint of pink, which gains in intensity in the second half of summer, and the shape, too, can change from a wide, shallow cup to a rosette. Prune the stems in late winter by one-half to two-thirds. Harder pruning gives fewer stems but larger flowers, while lighter pruning gives more flowering stems with slightly smaller blooms.

PLANT PROFILE

HEIGHT 3ft (90cm)

SPREAD 3½ft (1.1m)

TYPE Shrub

HARDINESS Z5–9

FLOWERING Summer

E | EYE PAINT ('Maceye')

EYE PAINT IS AN APPROPRIATELY VIVID NAME for this rose because the clusters (in varying sizes) of bright red, open flowers have a neat white eye, with yellow stamens right in the middle. Healthy, disease-free, and free-flowering, there is a profusion of blooms and glossy foliage, making EYE PAINT an excellent choice for a front-of-border position, or even a colorful, low dividing hedge across the middle of the garden. Cut back the main stems in late winter to 10–18in (25–45cm), and reduce the sideshoots by about one-third of their length.

PLANT PROFILE

HEIGHT 3½ft (1.1m)

SPREAD 2½ft (75cm)

TYPE Bush (cluster-flowered)

HARDINESS Z5–9

FLOWERING Summer to autumn

'Fantin-Latour'

F

A FAVORITE AMONG THE ROSE EXPERTS, 'Fantin-Latour' was introduced in 1900. It makes a solid shrub, well covered in sweet-scented, petal-packed, large pink flowers, and has its one burst of bloom in midsummer. The dark green, leafy growth gives it extra presence and shape. A Centifolia rose, it is named after 19th-century French artist Henri Fantin-Latour. Prune to maintain its impressive shrub shape, removing only diseased, dead, and damaged growth, and leaving the old wood intact. Give a minimal late-winter pruning to promote a balanced shape.

PLANT PROFILE

HEIGHT	5ft (1.5m)
SPREAD	4ft (1.2m)
TYPE	Old garden rose
HARDINESS	Z4–9 H9–1
FLOWERING	Midsummer

F

'Félicité Parmentier'

WHAT MARKS OUT THIS TOUGH, SCENTED rose is the way its buds fatten and fatten, with a slight yellow tinge, and then open to reveal a tightly packed arrangement of light pink petals with a touch of cream at the edges. The shape is upright and compact, and the green leaves have a grayish tinge. An Alba rose, it needs very little attention. To create a large, impressive shrub, remove only diseased, dead, and damaged growth. Give a light trim in late winter to help produce a balanced shape and plenty of flowering stems with smaller blooms. Harder pruning gives fewer stems with larger flowers.

PLANT PROFILE

HEIGHT 4½ft (1.3m)

SPREAD 4ft (1.2m)

TYPE Old garden rose

HARDINESS Z3–9 H9–3

FLOWERING Midsummer

'Félicité Perpétue'

AN EXCELLENT OLD RAMBLING ROSE, dating back to 1827, this is still a best buy. The prolific small flowers, 1½in (4cm) wide, make a great show of white against the dark green foliage. The growth is vigorous and bushy, forming an impenetrable shape, just right for growing into a sturdy tree or hedge, over an old wall, or for covering an eyesore. It also grows on cold, shady walls. 'Félicité Perpétue' can even be allowed to mound up on the ground. For the first two years, prune sideshoots in late summer by 3in (8cm) to a strong, new shoot. From then on, prune up to one-third of the oldest main stems to the ground.

PLANT PROFILE

HEIGHT	To 15ft (5m)
TYPE	Rambler
HARDINESS	Z6–9 H9–6
FLOWERING	Midsummer

F

FELLOWSHIP ('Harwelcome')

AN EXTREMELY RELIABLE ROSE, FELLOWSHIP keeps flowering with incredible freedom all through summer, and rarely presents any problems. The deep orange flowers are not too flashy, and they add a distinctive, colorful note to a mixed rose garden or border. Even the leaves are healthy and glossy. It is an excellent present for someone completely lacking a green thumb. Prune in late winter, cutting back the main stems to 10–18in (25–45cm) above the ground and shortening the sideshoots by approximately one-third.

PLANT PROFILE

HEIGHT	30in (75cm)
SPREAD	24in (60cm)
TYPE	Bush (cluster-flowered)
HARDINESS	Z5–9
FLOWERING	Summer to autumn

'Ferdinand Pichard'

F

RED- AND PINK-STRIPED PETALS might sound horribly garish, but with its pale pink background, this Hybrid Perpetual rose actually looks like a subtle raspberry ripple ice cream. The effect is balanced by the glossy leaves, while the shape is upright and compact. There is one main flush of richly scented flowers in early summer, with many more following after. In formal gardens, prune shoots by one-half to two-thirds in late winter. In less formal and cottage gardens, remove only diseased, dead, and damaged growth, and give a light overall pruning for shape.

PLANT PROFILE

HEIGHT 5ft (1.5m)
SPREAD 4ft (1.2m)
TYPE Old garden rose
HARDINESS Z5–9
FLOWERING Summer to autumn

F

FERDY ('Keitoli')

FINE-CUT LEAVES COVER THE ARCHING STEMS, and make a mound of uneven growth, which is quite spectacular when it erupts in flowers in summer. The blooms are small and tightly packed together and give a frothy, bright pink effect. FERDY is particularly effective beside an artificial pond where you want a colorful, naturalistic look, and is also good at smothering weeds. Little pruning is needed, but if growth is getting too rampant, cut back each overlong stem to an outward-facing bud in late winter. Shorten sideshoots at the same time if necessary.

PLANT PROFILE

HEIGHT 32in (80cm)

SPREAD 4ft (1.2m)

TYPE Groundcover

HARDINESS Z5–9

FLOWERING Summer to autumn

FESTIVAL ('Kordialo')

F

WINNER OF SOME PRESTIGIOUS ROSE PRIZES, including UK Rose of the Year in 1994, FESTIVAL is highly regarded for the silver color on the underside of its petals, which are crimson-scarlet on top, and also for its abundant, luxuriant, dark green leaves. Give it a prominent position, possibly in a pot, near a focal point such as the base of a statue, where it adds a flashy touch. In late winter, remove all growth apart from the strongest shoots, and then cut them back by one-third to one-half. This forces up plenty of new, vigorous growth.

PLANT PROFILE	
HEIGHT	24in (60cm)
SPREAD	20in (50cm)
TYPE	Bush (cluster-flowered, patio)
HARDINESS	Z5–9
FLOWERING	Summer to autumn

filipes 'Kiftsgate'

A FANTASTICALLY RAMPANT GROWER, *R. filipes* 'Kiftsgate' can be thought of as impressively power-packed or manically over the top. Try it only if you have lots of space because it cannot be restrained. It is normally grown high into a tree, from where it often launches into adjacent trees. It can also be roughly trained around a garden boundary, where its vicious thorns make an impenetrable barrier. The stunning summer display involves thousands of small, creamy white flowers. Pruning is not necessary, but you can cut one-third of the oldest main stems to ground level annually.

PLANT PROFILE
HEIGHT To 30ft (10m)
TYPE Rambler
HARDINESS Z6–9 H9–6
FLOWERING Midsummer; hips in autumn

FRAGRANT CLOUD ('Tanellis')

F

THE SCENT IS SUPERB, the flower shape stylish, the color stays coral red and hardly fades, and the foliage is glossy, dark green. In short, FRAGRANT CLOUD is a real winner, with the first buds opening in early summer. Grow it for the show bench and garden, where it can also be trained as a standard. The only minor drawbacks are possible attacks of mildew and blackspot. In late winter, remove all unproductive stems, and prune hard to outward-facing buds at 8–10in (20–25cm). This helps deter shoots from crowding the center. For large, showy flowers, prune harder, to just two or three buds.

PLANT PROFILE

HEIGHT	30in (75cm)
SPREAD	24in (60cm)
TYPE	Bush (large-flowered)
HARDINESS	Z4–11 H12–1
FLOWERING	Summer to autumn

F | 'Francis E. Lester'

THE RATHER LAX, VIGOROUS, THORNY STEMS are usually grown into sturdy trees, or they can be trained through a mixed hedge. 'Francis E. Lester' is also good for covering an eyesore because it is hard to beat for sheer flower power and scent. The pink buds open to white flowers with yellow stamens. The abundant, dark green foliage is another plus. For the first two years, prune sideshoots by 3in (8cm) to a vigorous shoot in late summer. From the third year, prune up to one-third of the oldest main stems to ground level.

PLANT PROFILE

HEIGHT 15ft (5m)

TYPE Rambler

HARDINESS Z4–9

FLOWERING Midsummer; hips in autumn

'François Juranville'

A TALL RAMBLER, 'François Juranville' is perfect for sending up into large, sturdy trees and covering old, ugly sheds. It is extremely vigorous, with few thorns and decent-sized flowers. The blooms have a slightly deeper pink tinge in the center, and give off the scent of fresh apples. Do not be tempted to try it against a small wall because, as one of the most rampant ramblers, it is almost impossible to restrain. In late summer, for the first two years, prune sideshoots by 3in (8cm) to a strong, new shoot. From the third year onward, prune at most one-third of the oldest main stems back to ground level.

PLANT PROFILE	
HEIGHT 20ft (6m)	
TYPE Rambler	
HARDINESS Z5–9	
FLOWERING Midsummer	

F

'Frau Karl Druschki'

ONE OF THE BEST AND MOST BEAUTIFUL WHITES, 'Frau Karl Druschki' is a Hybrid Perpetual rose dating back to 1901 and has everything going for it except scent. The buds suggest red flowers because they have a red tinge, but they actually open to milky white. Growth is strong and arching, but look out for mildew. It is also known as 'Snow Queen' and 'White American Beauty'. In formal gardens, prune shoots by one-half to two-thirds in late winter. In less formal and cottage gardens, remove only diseased, dead, and damaged growth, and give a light overall pruning for shape.

PLANT PROFILE

HEIGHT To 5ft (1.5m)

SPREAD 4ft (1.2m)

TYPE Old garden rose

HARDINESS Z4–9

FLOWERING Summer to autumn

FREEDOM ('Dicjem')

IF YOU NEED A PROLIFIC SHOW of bright yellow, scented roses all summer at the front of the border or in a mixed rose plan, this is the rose to go for. It is disease-resistant, vigorous, and bushy, and its rich color does not fade. Thoroughly reliable, this is a good choice for a new gardener. In late winter, remove all unproductive stems, and prune hard to outward-facing buds, leaving 8–10in (20–25cm) of stem. This helps to keep the center of the bush clear of crossing shoots. For large, showy flowers, prune harder, leaving just two or three buds on each stem.

F

PLANT PROFILE

HEIGHT 30in (75cm)

SPREAD 24in (60cm)

TYPE Bush (large-flowered)

HARDINESS Z5–9 H9–5

FLOWERING Summer to autumn

F

'Fritz Nobis'

A SHAPELY SHRUB WITH A BIG REPUTATION, 'Fritz Nobis' provides an excellent show of clear pink flowers that hang on for a long time in early summer when it is at its peak. Few shrub roses equal its display. These factors, with the large, dark green leaves, vigorous growth, autumn-to-winter show of hips, and gentle scent, make 'Fritz Nobis' a high-class shrub. Remove only diseased, dead, and damaged growth when pruning. Give a late-winter trim to help produce a balanced shape. Harder pruning gives fewer stems with larger flowers, lighter pruning more flowering stems with smaller blooms.

PLANT PROFILE

HEIGHT 6ft (2m)

SPREAD 6ft (2m)

TYPE Shrub

HARDINESS Z5–9

FLOWERING Summer; hips in autumn to winter

'Fru Dagmar Hastrup'

ONE OF THE BEST OF THE RUGOSA ROSES, 'Fru Dagmar Hastrup' has compact, shrubby growth, dark green leaves, rich pink buds, light pink flowers, and crimson hips. The effectiveness of the red hips is highlighted because they coincide with the final burst of flowers. 'Fru Dagmar Hastrup' is very effective in borders, but it also makes an excellent, low-growing, colorful hedge, which is how many prefer to grow it. In late winter, prune by one-half to two-thirds. Pruning harder gives fewer stems with larger flowers, while pruning more lightly gives more flowering stems with smaller blooms.

PLANT PROFILE

HEIGHT 3ft (1m)

SPREAD 4ft (1.2m)

TYPE Shrub

HARDINESS Z2–9 H9–1

FLOWERING Summer; hips in autumn

F 'Frühlingsgold'

A TOP CHOICE FOR A PALE YELLOW ROSE, 'Frühlingsgold' has a wonderful, heavy scent, and can flower from late spring or early summer. It is tough and reliable, with arching branches covered from base to tip with flowers that gradually fade to white. Although it flowers for only a few weeks early in the season, it does provide one of the best rose sights of the year. Remove only diseased, dead, and damaged growth when pruning to preserve its shrubby appearance. A minimal late-winter pruning also helps to maintain a balanced shape.

PLANT PROFILE

HEIGHT	8ft (2.5m)
SPREAD	7ft (2.2m)
TYPE	Shrub
HARDINESS	Z4–9
FLOWERING	Late spring to early summer

'Frühlingsmorgen'

F

THE SPRAYS OF LARGE, SCENTED FLOWERS are light pink with primrose yellow stamens in the center, and a dash of maroon. While the main flush is in early summer, you will get extra flowers toward the end of summer, followed by a few large red hips on the bushy growth. In late winter, cut out diseased, dead, and damaged growth. Give a light pruning at the same time for a balanced shape. If you prune harder, the rose will produce fewer stems with larger flowers.

PLANT PROFILE

HEIGHT 6ft (2m)

SPREAD 5ft (1.5m)

TYPE Shrub

HARDINESS Z4–9 H9–4

FLOWERING Early and late summer; hips in autumn

G | *gallica* var. *officinalis* Apothecary's rose, Red rose of Lancaster

THIS ANCIENT GALLICA ROSE, dating back to the Middle Ages and one of the oldest still grown in Europe, is a beautiful midsummer highlight. The prickle-free stems carry pinkish red flowers, either individually or in clusters of two to four, set against dark green leaves, and followed by orange-red hips. It sometimes suffers from mildew. In late winter, remove only diseased, dead, and damaged growth, leaving the old wood intact. If necessary, prune lightly to encourage a balanced shape. Harder pruning gives fewer stems with larger flowers.

PLANT PROFILE

HEIGHT 32in (80cm)

SPREAD 3ft (1m)

TYPE Old garden rose

HARDINESS Z3–9 H9–1

FLOWERING Midsummer; hips in autumn

gallica 'Versicolor' Rosa mundi

G

THIS RED- AND PINK-STRIPED ROSE from the 17th century is said to get its name from King Henry II's mistress, Fair Rosamund. Small and showy, it can be grown alone or in a row as a mini-hedge, injecting color into formal and informal plans. It belongs to the Gallica group of roses, which flower only once in the summer and give a high-impact display. It is richly scented. Prune lightly in late winter, removing only diseased, dead, and damaged wood and, if necessary, trimming the rest back for a balanced shape. If you want fewer stems with larger flowers, prune the stems harder.

PLANT PROFILE

HEIGHT 32in (80cm)

SPREAD 3ft (1m)

TYPE Old garden rose

HARDINESS Z3–9 H9–1

FLOWERING Midsummer

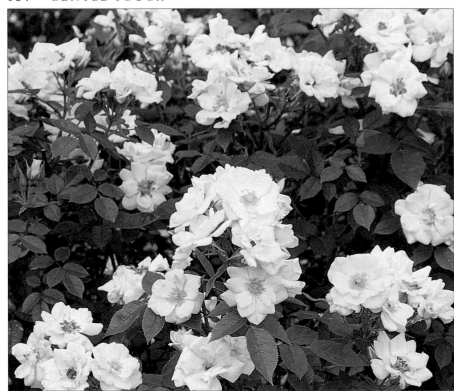

G | GENTLE TOUCH ('Diclulu')

IDEAL FOR GROWING IN SMALL GARDENS, in pots, or as edging, this delicate rose has gentle sprays of pale salmon-colored flowers. Each bloom is about 2in (5cm) wide and beautifully shaped, with a high-pointed bud. The dark green leaves help highlight the flowers, which appear all through the summer season. In late winter, prune away all growth except for the strongest shoots. Cut these back by one-third to one-half to force up plenty of new growth and maintain vigor.

PLANT PROFILE	
HEIGHT 20in (50cm)	
SPREAD 16in (40cm)	
TYPE Bush (cluster-flowered, patio)	
HARDINESS Z5–9	
FLOWERING Summer to autumn	

GERTRUDE JEKYLL ('Ausbord')

G

GERTRUDE JEKYLL SCORES HIGHER POINTS for its individual flowers than its overall shape. The rich, pink blooms are large and heavy (opening from small buds), and have a strong scent, but they tend to hang down in the rain. While the growth is not exactly neat, it is strong, disease-resistant, and repeat-flowering, making a first-class rose. It is perfect for the back of the border. While the rose is dormant, prune shoots by one-half to two-thirds. Pruning more lightly gives more flowering stems with smaller blooms, while harder pruning gives fewer stems with larger flowers.

PLANT PROFILE

HEIGHT	5ft (1.5m)
SPREAD	3ft (1m)
TYPE	Shrub
HARDINESS	Z5–9
FLOWERING	Summer to autumn

G | GLAD TIDINGS ('Tantide')

THE GROWTH IS BUSHY AND UPRIGHT, and the long-lasting flowers are beautifully shaped, with a striking, bright crimson color. There are plenty of buds giving excellent coverage. Groups of around four or five of these bushes make a striking sight. If you do not mind virtually scentless roses, GLAD TIDINGS has a lot of pluses. Blackspot may be a nuisance, but it can be tackled by spraying. In late winter, cut back the main stems to 10–18in (25–45cm) above the ground, and reduce sideshoots by one-third.

PLANT PROFILE

HEIGHT 32in (80cm)

SPREAD 26in (65cm)

TYPE Bush (cluster-flowered)

HARDINESS Z5–9

FLOWERING Summer to autumn

glauca

G

EXTREMELY POPULAR, THIS ROSE HAS HEIGHT, grace, and lightness, shooting up out of the ground and then arching over. It has virtually thornless stems and an often open, see-through effect. The leaves are as good as the flowers, being gray-green in light shade (more coppery in direct sun), while the small, gentle pink flowers are single with a white center. The hips are brownish red. *R. glauca* adds to the flow of borders, unlike those high-profile roses that hog the limelight so that you barely look beyond them. Pruning is unnecessary except for minor trimming for shape.

PLANT PROFILE
HEIGHT 6ft (2m)
SPREAD 5ft (1.5m)
TYPE Wild
HARDINESS Z2–8 H8–1
FLOWERING Midsummer; hips in autumn

G 'Glenfiddich'

ONE OF THE TOP YELLOWS among the cluster-flowered bush roses, 'Glenfiddich' keeps flowering over a long period. The growth is bushy with dark green leaves, and the flowers (which are also good for cutting) appear on straight stems, either individually or grouped in sprays; their amber-enriched color almost matches the whiskey after which 'Glenfiddich' is named. It is a reliable and disease-free rose. Prune in late winter, cutting back the main stems to 10–18in (25–45cm), and shorten sideshoots by about one-third.

PLANT PROFILE

HEIGHT	32in (80cm)
SPREAD	24in (60cm)
TYPE	Bush (cluster-flowered)
HARDINESS	Z5–9 H9–5
FLOWERING	Summer to autumn

'Gloire de Dijon' Old glory rose

ESSENTIAL IN A COTTAGE GARDEN because it has some of the genes of an old garden rose, 'Gloire de Dijon' sends up vigorous stems covered in fat buds in early summer. The large buff-yellow flowers (with a touch of pink) have a strong, rich scent. After the first main burst of flowers, more follow, giving a constant show. Bend down the first stems to force up new growth and prevent the rose from being bare low down. Do not prune for the first two years, but from then on, prune in the autumn, after flowering, nipping back the main stems if they are too long and shortening sideshoots by two-thirds.

PLANT PROFILE	
HEIGHT	15ft (5m)
TYPE	Climber
HARDINESS	Z5–9 H9–5
FLOWERING	Summer to autumn

G | ## GOLDEN CELEBRATION ('Ausgold')

ONE OF THE BEST YELLOWS AT THIS HEIGHT, this rose has nothing but good qualities—a gentle arching shape, vigorous growth, disease resistance, and very large, strongly scented flowers with a rich color. GOLDEN CELEBRATION makes an attractive centerpiece in any bed. To enhance its impressive shrub shape, remove only diseased, dead, and damaged growth, and leave the old wood intact. Give a minimal pruning in late winter for a balanced outline. If you prune harder, fewer stems with larger flowers will result; lighter pruning produces more flowering stems with smaller blooms.

PLANT PROFILE

HEIGHT 4ft (1.2m)

SPREAD 4ft (1.2m)

TYPE Shrub

HARDINESS Z5–9

FLOWERING Summer

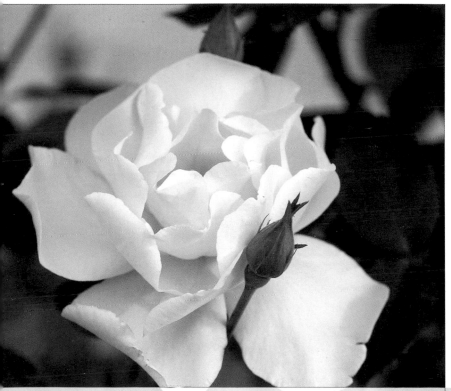

'Golden Showers'

THE SCENTED YELLOW FLOWERS of 'Golden Showers' give a remarkably continuous show all summer, backed up by the glossy foliage. Growth is not that high, making it ideal for average-size walls and posts. Train it around and up posts, or out horizontally along walls to force up new growth; if 'Golden Showers' is allowed to grow straight up, the lower growth will be bare, with all the flowers high at the top. Allow the plant to establish by not pruning for the first two years, but then start to prune in the autumn, after flowering, cutting back the main stems and shortening sideshoots by two-thirds.

PLANT PROFILE
HEIGHT 10ft (3m)
TYPE Climber
HARDINESS Z5–9 H9–5
FLOWERING Summer to autumn

G | GOLDEN WEDDING ('Arokris')

FLOWERING ALL THROUGH THE SUMMER, this rose is equally reliable outside and indoors as a cut flower. The blooms are on the large side, being stylish, bright, and showy, while the foliage is attractively glossy. The bushy, vigorous growth compensates for the lack of any discernible scent. These excellent qualities mean that the popularity of GOLDEN WEDDING is not due just to its name, though it does make a very good anniversary gift. In late winter, cut back the main stems to 10–18in (25–45cm), and reduce the sideshoots by about one-third of their length.

PLANT PROFILE

HEIGHT 3ft (1m)

SPREAD 30in (75cm)

TYPE Bush (cluster-flowered)

HARDINESS Z6–9

FLOWERING Summer

'Golden Wings'

WITH AN OPEN, SAUCERLIKE SHAPE, the flowers of GOLDEN WINGS have an amber center surrounded by 5–10 pale yellow petals. They withstand inclement weather and keep appearing all through summer if the old ones are promptly removed as they fade. The scent is often described as delicious and refreshing. This rose is disease-resistant and totally reliable. Pruning is minimal. Remove only diseased, dead, and damaged growth, and leave the old wood intact. Cut back overlong shoots in late winter for a balanced shape. If you prune harder, the result will be fewer stems with larger flowers.

PLANT PROFILE	
HEIGHT	5ft (1.5m)
SPREAD	4½ft (1.3m)
TYPE	Shrub
HARDINESS	Z4–9 H9–1
FLOWERING	Summer to autumn

G | 'Goldfinch'

A GOOD CHOICE OF RAMBLER if you don't want one that
shoots out in all directions, making tangled growth in trees.
'Goldfinch' is much more restrained, being valued for its
thornless stems, glossy leaves, deep yellow flowers fading to
white, and fruity scent. It makes a lovely addition to a mixed
hedge, though it can also be grown as a large shrub. For the
first two years only, in late summer, prune sideshoots by 3in
(8cm) to a strong, new shoot. From then on, prune at most
one-third of the oldest main stems back to ground level.

PLANT PROFILE

HEIGHT 8ft (2.5m)

TYPE Rambler

HARDINESS Z5–9 H9–5

FLOWERING Midsummer

GRAHAM THOMAS ('Ausmas')

A HIGHLY VALUED ROSE named after a great rose expert, GRAHAM THOMAS has a long list of attractions. It combines pure yellow flowers with the look of an old garden rose, a deep scent, vigorous, upright growth, and a flowering season lasting from early summer into the start of autumn. It makes an excellent centerpiece in a bed in formal and cottage gardens. In late winter, prune stems by one–half to two–thirds. The harder you prune, the fewer the stems and the larger the flowers; lighter pruning results in the reverse.

G

PLANT PROFILE

HEIGHT 4ft (1.2m)

SPREAD 5ft (1.5m)

TYPE Shrub

HARDINESS Z5–9 H9–5

FLOWERING Summer to autumn

G | 'Grandpa Dickson'

QUITE A SHORT, UPRIGHT PLANT, this takes up very little space with its large, shapely, pale yellow flowers. It can easily be incorporated in any plan with annuals, and keeps the planting alive with its long flowering season. 'Grandpa Dickson' withstands bad weather but lacks only one thing: a decent scent. To encourage plenty of new shoots and an open-centered bush shape, prune in late winter by removing all unproductive stems, and cutting hard to outward-facing buds at 8–10in (20–25cm). For large, showy flowers, prune harder, leaving just two or three buds.

PLANT PROFILE

HEIGHT	30in (75cm)
SPREAD	24in (60cm)
TYPE	Bush (large-flowered)
HARDINESS	Z5–9 H9–5
FLOWERING	Summer to autumn

'Great Maiden's Blush'

A LARGE, BRANCHING, ARCHING SHRUB for the back of
the border or an informal perimeter hedge, 'Great Maiden's
Blush' has gray-green leaves and a gentle pink color on
opening, fading to pinkish white. It gives a substantial show
in the middle of the summer, when the scent is more sweet
and refined than strong. It is listed under Alba roses in most
catalogs. Remove only diseased, dead, and damaged growth
when pruning, and cut back lightly in late winter to produce
a balanced shape. Harder pruning gives fewer stems with
larger flowers.

PLANT PROFILE	
HEIGHT 6ft (2m)	
SPREAD 4½ft (1.3m)	
TYPE Old garden rose	
HARDINESS Z3–9 H9–1	
FLOWERING Midsummer	

G | GROUSE ('Korimro')

ALMOST THE ULTIMATE GROUNDCOVER ROSE, GROUSE does not get above knee-high and spreads out widely and rapidly in all directions. Unlike many so-called groundcover roses that have wide, gappy growth, this smothers any weeds beneath. The small flowers (appearing in mid- and late summer) are pale pink, verging on white, and the leaves glossy, dark green. GROUSE can also be grown to spread down banks and hang over walls. Little pruning is required, but if growth is too rampant, cut back to an outward-facing bud in late winter. Shorten sideshoots at the same time if necessary.

PLANT PROFILE

HEIGHT 24in (60cm)

SPREAD 10ft (3m)

TYPE Groundcover

HARDINESS Z5–9 H9–6

FLOWERING Summer

'Gruss an Aachen'

IT MAY BE ON THE SMALL SIDE, but 'Gruss an Aachen' certainly has high-quality flowers. They look like those of an old garden rose and start off light pink, gradually fading to soft creamy white. In addition, 'Gruss an Aachen' has a long flowering season and the scent is very good, making it an excellent choice for the front of a border. Despite having been around since 1909, it is still not that widely grown, but it is well worth trying, especially in small gardens. In late winter, cut back main stems to 10–18in (25–45cm) above the ground, and reduce sideshoots by about one-third of their length.

PLANT PROFILE	
HEIGHT 2½ft (75cm)	
SPREAD 3ft (1m)	
TYPE Bush (cluster-flowered)	
HARDINESS Z5–9	
FLOWERING Summer to autumn	

G | 'Guinée'

IF YOU WANT LARGE, DARK RED FLOWERS and a terrific scent, this climber scores very highly. The early summer flush of blooms is the best. Plant it where you can appreciate the scent and, for the best effect, give it a light background and pamper it with rich soil. For the first two years, simply train new shoots into a horizontal position to produce flowering sideshoots. From the third year, prune in the autumn, after flowering, nipping back the main stems if they are too long, and shortening sideshoots by two-thirds.

PLANT PROFILE

HEIGHT	15ft (5m)
TYPE	Climber
HARDINESS	Z5–9 H9–5
FLOWERING	Summer

'Hakuun'

H

A VERY USEFUL EDGING PLANT with bushy growth, 'Hakuun' can also be grown in pots. There are dozens of more recent patio roses (this is a 1962 introduction), but most tend to be brightly colored reds or soft, quiet pinks, making this white still a good buy. The flowers have an orange-yellow tinge on opening, which quickly fades to creamy white (the translation of the Japanese word *hakuun* is "white cloud"). Prune in late winter, selecting the strongest shoots and removing the rest. Shorten the selected shoots by one-third to one-half to force up plenty of new, vigorous growth.

PLANT PROFILE

HEIGHT	16in (40cm)
SPREAD	18in (45cm)
TYPE	Bush (cluster-flowered, patio)
HARDINESS	Z5–9
FLOWERING	Summer to autumn

H | HAMPSHIRE ('Korhamp')

A MODEST GROUNDCOVER ROSE, HAMPSHIRE makes a knee-high, spreading mound covered with 2in- (5cm-) wide, open, scarlet flowers. They have a striking yellow center that gradually fades to white. HAMPSHIRE also offers a long flowering season, glossy leaves, and an attractive display of orange hips. Little pruning is needed, but if growth is getting too rampant, cut back stems to an outward-facing bud in late winter. At the same time, shorten the sideshoots if they are becoming too long.

PLANT PROFILE

HEIGHT 12in (30cm)

SPREAD 30in (75cm)

TYPE Groundcover

HARDINESS Z5–9

FLOWERING Summer to autumn; hips in autumn

HANDEL ('Macha')

IDEAL FOR PILLARS AND POSTS and growing up small arches, this superb mini-climber reaches 10ft (3m). The almost scentless flowers are creamy white and stand out because they are pink around the edge. In the hottest part of summer, the pink color tends to intensify and sometimes even spreads. After the first main crop of flowers, the display continues. For the first two years, train new shoots into a horizontal position. From the third year onward, prune in autumn, after flowering, nipping back the main stems if necessary and shortening sideshoots by two-thirds.

PLANT PROFILE

HEIGHT 10ft (3m)

TYPE Climber

HARDINESS Z5–9 H9–5

FLOWERING Summer to autumn

H HANNAH GORDON ('Korweiso')

SLIGHTLY SMALLER THAN MOST ROSES in this category, HANNAH GORDON makes an attractive, bushy plant with a spreading, open shape well covered in dark green leaves. The buds are plump, the flowers large, the scent delicate, and the sprays keep appearing all summer. It is a very useful rose at the front of a bed or border, though it can also be grown in a large tub or urn in a courtyard garden. In late winter, cut back the main stems to 10–18in (25–45cm) above the ground, and prune sideshoots by about one-third of their length.

PLANT PROFILE

HEIGHT	32in (80cm)
SPREAD	26in (65cm)
TYPE	Bush (cluster-flowered)
HARDINESS	Z4–11 H12–1
FLOWERING	Summer to autumn

'Harry Wheatcroft'

H

FUN, EVEN OUTRAGEOUS, this brightly colored rose has a mix of red, yellow, and orange stripes and streaks on its petals, while the undersides are yellow. Forget the lack of scent and the tendency to mildew; this is a brash rose with a high-pointed flower shape before it fully opens, and the ability to withstand rain. The leaves are glossy, reddish green. In late winter, remove all unproductive stems, and prune the rest hard to outward-facing buds, leaving 8–10in (20–25cm) of stem. This helps discourage crisscrossing shoots in the center. For large, showy flowers, prune harder, to just two or three buds.

PLANT PROFILE

HEIGHT	3ft (1m)
SPREAD	24in (60cm)
TYPE	Bush (large-flowered)
HARDINESS	Z5–9
FLOWERING	Summer to autumn

H 'Henri Martin' Red moss rose

A GOOD CHOICE FOR A SHADY, COLD WALL, although it performs far better in the sun, 'Henri Martin' has lovely, 3in- (8cm-) wide, scented flowers of the richest near-crimson red. The growth is arching, graceful, and nearly thorn-free, with dark green leaves. 'Henri Martin' is listed in many catalogs with the Moss roses because of the attractive, small, mosslike growth on the stems and buds. Remove only diseased, dead, and damaged growth, and give a minimal late-winter pruning for shape. Harder pruning gives fewer stems with larger flowers, lighter pruning more stems with smaller blooms.

PLANT PROFILE

HEIGHT To 6ft (2m)

SPREAD 4ft (1.2m)

TYPE Old garden rose

HARDINESS Z4–9 H9–1

FLOWERING Summer

HERITAGE ('Ausblush)

GROWING SATISFYINGLY, BUSHILY UPRIGHT, this rose has cupped, light pink, lemon-scented flowers that are almost white at the edge. The flowers keep appearing over the summer, with some still hanging on in autumn, and the stems are virtually thorn-free. HERITAGE adds a strong presence to pastel color schemes because of its large, 4½in- (11cm-) wide flowers. In late winter, prune shoots by one-half to two-thirds. Pruning hard gives fewer stems with larger flowers, while pruning more lightly results in more flowering stems with smaller blooms.

H

PLANT PROFILE	
HEIGHT 4ft (1.2m)	
SPREAD 4ft (1.2m)	
TYPE Shrub	
HARDINESS Z5–9	
FLOWERING Summer to autumn	

H | 'Hermosa'

AN EXQUISITE, MEDIUM-SIZED CHINA ROSE dating back to
1840, 'Hermosa' is known for its small, pale pink, lightly
scented flowers with 35 petals. They keep appearing over a
long period from summer to autumn. The buds are high-
pointed and attractive, appearing on bushy growth with just
a few prickles and gray-green leaves. To make any impact in
large plans, it needs to be planted in groups of three or more.
When pruning, remove only diseased, dead, and damaged
growth, and leave the old wood intact. A minimal late-winter
pruning also helps produce a balanced shape.

PLANT PROFILE

HEIGHT 3ft (1m)

SPREAD 24in (60cm)

TYPE Old garden rose

HARDINESS Z6–9

FLOWERING Summer to autumn

HERTFORDSHIRE ('Kortenay')

H

HERTFORDSHIRE WILL NICELY FILL A BORDER GAP with its flat, wide-open pink flowers, which are yellow in the center, set against bright green leaves. Growth is quite dense and will block out weeds after two to three seasons when it has had a chance to really fill out. Initially, though, you will have to weed under and around it, but note that it is quite prickly. It has good disease resistance. Little pruning is needed, but if growth is too rampant, cut it back to outward-facing buds in late winter. Shorten sideshoots at the same time if necessary.

PLANT PROFILE

HEIGHT 18in (45cm)

SPREAD 3ft (1m)

TYPE Groundcover

HARDINESS Z5–9

FLOWERING Summer to autumn

H | HIGH HOPES ('Haryup')

WITH BEAUTIFUL, SHAPELY FLOWERS and a sweet scent over a long period, HIGH HOPES is a fairly recent (1992), highly successful introduction. It is perfect for a medium-high doorway, arch, pillar, or pergola. Growth is quite flexible and easily trained, modest, and will not romp away in a tangled mess; it gives decent results even in relatively poor conditions. Avoid pruning for the first two years, but train new shoots horizontally to produce flowering sideshoots. From then on, prune in the autumn, after flowering, cutting back the main stems as needed and shortening sideshoots by two-thirds.

PLANT PROFILE

HEIGHT 12ft (4m)

TYPE Climber

HARDINESS Z5–9 H9–5

FLOWERING Summer to autumn

ICEBERG ('Korbin')

I

AN EXTREMELY POPULAR ROSE, it provides continuous flowers all summer and into autumn. The buds have a pink tinge but the flowers are actually clear white. Anyone who snobbishly thinks a popular rose must be completely lacking in style is totally wrong when it comes to ICEBERG. Plant it among beautiful red and pink roses and you will get an excellent combination. In late winter, cut back the main stems to 10–18in (25–45cm) above ground, and shorten sideshoots by about one-third. ICEBERG can also be grown as a standard, and there is a climbing version, reaching about 10ft (3m) high.

PLANT PROFILE

HEIGHT	32in (80cm)
SPREAD	26in (65cm)
TYPE	Bush (cluster-flowered)
HARDINESS	Z5–9 H9–5
FLOWERING	Summer to autumn

I   INGRID BERGMAN ('Poulman')

THE RED FLOWERS ARE DARK, the petals velvety, the scent refreshing, and the leaves dark green and leathery. In addition, new buds keep appearing all summer long on the strong, branching growth. INGRID BERGMAN, introduced in 1984, is a good performer and provides superb, sumptuous blooms for cut-flower displays. Prune in late winter, removing unproductive stems altogether, and cut back the remainder to outward-pointing buds at 8–10in (20–25cm). This helps to eliminate crossing shoots in the center of the bush. For large, showy flowers, prune harder, to two or three buds.

PLANT PROFILE

HEIGHT	32in (80cm)
SPREAD	26in (65cm)
TYPE	Bush (large-flowered)
HARDINESS	Z5–9
FLOWERING	Summer to autumn

INTRIGUE ('Korlech')

SMALL, BUSHY, AND UPRIGHT, INTRIGUE has dark red, citrus-scented flowers. If you like the initial high-pointed flower shape of large-flowered bush roses, and want them in big numbers, try this rose. The blooms appear in clusters all summer and beyond, and are great for cutting. The leaves are glossy, purplish red. INTRIGUE guarantees good color at the front of a border. Cut back the main stems to 10–18in (25–45cm) above the ground in late winter, and shorten sideshoots by about one-third.

PLANT PROFILE	
HEIGHT 28in (70cm)	
SPREAD 24in (60cm)	
TYPE Bush (cluster-flowered)	
HARDINESS Z5–9	
FLOWERING Summer to autumn	

I

I

INVINCIBLE ('Runatru')

A SMALL BUSH ROSE with glossy, dark green foliage and
clusters of bright crimson flowers all summer long, this looks
as good in the garden as it does when brightening up cut-
flower displays. If you need a medium-high red, it will not let
you down. The overall shape is bushy and compact, and the
leaves are disease-resistant. In late winter, cut back the main
stems to 10–18in (25–45cm), and reduce the sideshoots by
about one-third of their length.

PLANT PROFILE

HEIGHT 28in (70cm)

SPREAD 20in (50cm)

TYPE Bush (cluster-flowered)

HARDINESS Z5–9

FLOWERING Summer to autumn

'Ispahan'

I

'ISPAHAN' HAS ONE OF THE LONGEST DISPLAYS of any old garden rose, and mixes clusters of clear pink flowers with a lovely scent. At 5ft (1.5m) high, this Damask rose is usually grown toward the back of the border and is superb in cottage and formal gardens. Growth is bushy and upright, and the stems are virtually thornless. When pruning, remove only diseased, dead, and damaged growth. A gentle trim in late winter also helps produce a balanced shape. Light pruning will produce more flowering stems with smaller blooms, while harder pruning gives fewer stems with larger flowers.

PLANT PROFILE

HEIGHT 5ft (1.5m)

SPREAD 4ft (1.2m)

TYPE Old garden rose

HARDINESS Z4–9 H9–1

FLOWERING Summer

J | JACQUELINE DU PRÉ ('Harwanna')

WITH ITS WIDE-OPEN FLOWERS set against dark green, glossy leaves, this rose provides color all through the growing season. The golden-centered flowers never let up, growth is bushy and vigorous, and if only the gentle scent were stronger JACQUELINE DU PRÉ would have everything. Still, it is a high-performance shrub for any garden. Prune out diseased, dead, and damaged growth, and leave the old wood intact. Give a minimal late-winter pruning to help produce a balanced shape; the harder you prune, the fewer the stems, but the larger the blooms.

PLANT PROFILE	
HEIGHT 4ft (1.2m)	
SPREAD 3ft (1m)	
TYPE Shrub	
HARDINESS Z5–9 H9–5	
FLOWERING Early summer to autumn	

'Julia's Rose'

J

THE COLOR IS EXTREMELY UNUSUAL, being a mix of copper and faded brown, and is hard to pin down. 'Julia's Rose' is well worth trying, but do note that it needs pampering and a protected site, and the growth is spindly with sparse, reddish green leaves. In late winter, remove all the unproductive stems, and prune the rest hard to outward-facing buds at 8–10in (20–25cm). This discourages shoots from crowding the center. For large, showy flowers, prune harder, to two or three buds.

PLANT PROFILE	
HEIGHT	30in (75cm)
SPREAD	18in (45cm)
TYPE	Bush (large-flowered)
HARDINESS	Z5–9 H9–1
FLOWERING	Summer to autumn

'Just Joey'

VOTED THE WORLD'S FAVORITE ROSE in 1994, 'Just Joey' is a bright and breezy rose, still justifiably popular, and has a highly distinctive color, being copper-pink, even orange, with frilly edges. There is nothing precious about it, and it will flower reliably through and beyond summer, the blooms withstanding soaking downpours. When pruning, you are aiming for an open-centered bush shape. Remove unproductive stems in late winter and cut the remaining stems to outward-facing buds at 8–10in (20–25cm) from the ground. For large, showy flowers, prune harder, leaving just two or three buds.

PLANT PROFILE

HEIGHT 30in (75cm)

SPREAD 28in (70cm)

TYPE Bush (large-flowered)

HARDINESS Z5–7 H7–5

FLOWERING Summer to autumn

'Kathleen Harrop'

K

ITS CLUSTERS OF SCENTED, PALE PINK FLOWERS and thornless stems make this rose a very decent alternative to the slightly more vigorous, deep pink climber 'Zéphirine Drouhin' (*see page 314*), especially for a cold, shady site. Mildew can strike when it is against a wall; good air circulation is the solution. Train new shoots horizontally for the first two years. In the following years, prune after flowering, nipping back the main stems and shortening sideshoots by two-thirds. With pruning, it can be kept as an 8ft (2.5m) shrub: cut back shoots by one-half to two-thirds after flowering.

PLANT PROFILE	
HEIGHT 10ft (3m)	
TYPE Climber	
HARDINESS Z6–9 H9–6	
FLOWERING Summer to autumn	

K KATHRYN MORLEY ('Ausclub')

AN UPRIGHT ROSE combining repeat-flowering with the charm and scent of an old garden rose, KATHRYN MORLEY has flowers of soft pink petals held in a cupped shape. Just right for cottage gardens, it has gentle informality, vigorous growth, and an upright shape. It is the ideal ingredient in an easy-going, unobtrusive garden where there is plenty of color all summer. In late winter, prune shoots by one-half to two-thirds. Harder pruning gives fewer stems with larger flowers, lighter pruning more flowering stems with smaller blooms.

PLANT PROFILE

HEIGHT 3ft (1m)

SPREAD 3ft (1m)

TYPE Shrub

HARDINESS Z5–9

FLOWERING Summer

KEEPSAKE ('Kormalda')

K

THE RICH PINK FLOWERS OF KEEPSAKE will stand out in any garden, and withstand heavy rain. They are large, at 5in (12cm) wide, with a very faint scent, and make good cut flowers because they last well in water and have an attractive, even shape. If grown where there is shade in late afternoon, the pink of the flowers will appear even stronger. Its uneven, untidy growth gives it an informal, cottage-garden feel. In late winter, remove all unproductive stems, and prune the remainder hard to outward-facing buds at 8–10in (20–25cm). For large, showy flowers, prune harder, to two or three buds.

PLANT PROFILE

HEIGHT 30in (75cm)

SPREAD 24in (60cm)

TYPE Bush (large-flowered)

HARDINESS Z5–9 H9–5

FLOWERING Summer to autumn

K | KENT ('Poulcov')

PROLIFICALLY COVERED IN SMALL WHITE FLOWERS with a yellow eye, and tight-packed foliage, 'Kent' makes dense, bushy growth that will keep down weeds well or fill a small gap at the front of a border. Unlike some groundcover roses, it makes not an open, unpredictable sprawl but quite a neat, compact shape. It is never out of flower over summer. Minimal pruning is needed; if growth is getting too rampant, cut back the main shoots to outward-facing buds in late winter. Sideshoots can also be shortened then if necessary.

PLANT PROFILE

HEIGHT 18in (45cm)

SPREAD 3ft (1m)

TYPE Groundcover

HARDINESS Z5–9

FLOWERING Summer to autumn

'Königen von Dänemark'

K

ALSO KNOWN AS QUEEN OF DENMARK, this soft pink Alba rose makes a marvelous show in an old garden rose plan. The flowers open well clear of the foliage, their initial color is vivid red before turning pink, the scent is sweet, the leaves are blue-green, and the growth is upright and open. 'Königin von Dänemark' is very highly regarded by rose experts, and makes a fine midsummer show at the back of a border. When pruning in late winter, remove diseased, dead, and damaged growth, and trim to a balanced shape. If you prune harder, fewer stems with larger flowers will result.

PLANT PROFILE

HEIGHT 5ft (1.5m)

SPREAD 4ft (1.2m)

TYPE Old garden rose

HARDINESS Z3–9 H9–1

FLOWERING Midsummer

K 'Korresia'

GENERALLY CONSIDERED TO BE THE BEST YELLOW you can buy in this group of bush roses, 'Korresia' bears bright-colored flowers in sprays regularly over the summer. Each bloom is 3in (8cm) wide with wavy-edged petals and is lightly scented. With good disease resistance, 'Korresia' makes a good present for a novice gardener who needs high-performance plants that do not require any pampering. In late winter, cut back the main stems to 10–18in (25–45cm) above the ground, and shorten the sideshoots by about one-third.

PLANT PROFILE

HEIGHT 30in (75cm)

SPREAD 24in (60cm)

TYPE Bush (cluster-flowered)

HARDINESS Z5–9 H9–5

FLOWERING Summer to autumn

L. D. BRAITHWAITE ('Auscrim')

AN EXCELLENT, BRIGHT-RED–FLOWERING bushy plant,
L. D. BRAITHWAITE has a scent that is soft and lovely rather
than overpowering (being stronger when it is fully open). Its
uneven, loose growth is very much part of its appeal. It is
a strong performer that mixes well with old garden roses
and is nicely covered in flowers all summer. In late winter,
prune shoots by one-half to two-thirds. Harder pruning
gives fewer stems with larger flowers, and lighter pruning
more flowering stems with slightly smaller blooms.

L

PLANT PROFILE

HEIGHT 3½ft (1.1m)

SPREAD 3½ft (1.1m)

TYPE Shrub

HARDINESS Z5–9

FLOWERING Summer to autumn

L | L'AIMANT ('Harzola')

FREE-FLOWERING AND DISEASE-RESISTANT, L'AIMANT scores high points all around. Its flowers are a lovely, warm shade of pink with reddish overtones, making it stand out from other softer, quieter pinks. The scented flowers look equally delightful in the garden and in a cut-flower display, where it is particularly valued for its array of about 30 petals. Overall growth is vigorous and hard to fault. Cut back the main stems in late winter to 10–18in (25–45cm) above the ground, and reduce the sideshoots by about one-third of their length.

PLANT PROFILE

HEIGHT	3ft (1m)
SPREAD	30in (75cm)
TYPE	Bush (cluster-flowered)
HARDINESS	Z5–9
FLOWERING	Summer to autumn

LAURA FORD ('Chewarvel')

CALLING IT A CLIMBER might sound a bit ambitious for something that barely reaches past the scalp of a pro basketball player, but a climber it is, and just right for training up and around poles and the verticals on a pergola. The rich yellow flowers appear in clusters and have a faint fruity scent, while the leaves are glossy. If you need a restrained, brightly colored climber, it is a great choice. Do not prune for the first two years, but train new shoots into a horizontal position. From the third year on, prune after flowering, nipping back overlong main stems and shortening sideshoots by two-thirds.

PLANT PROFILE

HEIGHT	7ft (2.2m)
TYPE	Climber
HARDINESS	Z5–9 H9–5
FLOWERING	Summer to autumn

L

LEAPING SALMON ('Peamight')

WITH THE HIGH-POINTED FLOWER SHAPE of a large-flowered rose, LEAPING SALMON is 10ft (3m) tall, and just right for a pillar or arch. The scent is rich and sweet, the flowers are large and long-lasting when cut, and the glossy foliage is disease-resistant. The young stems need to be gently and horizontally trained against a wall when still young and flexible, before they quickly stiffen, to encourage more flowering shoots. From the third year onward, prune in the autumn, after flowering, nipping back the main stems if necessary and shortening sideshoots by two-thirds.

PLANT PROFILE	
HEIGHT 10ft (3m)	
TYPE Climber	
HARDINESS Z6–9	
FLOWERING Summer	

'Leverkusen'

L

A DUAL-PURPOSE, VIGOROUS, ARCHING CLIMBER, it can also be pruned and kept on the short side to make a very good shrub. Either way, it is known for its healthy, glossy leaves and clusters of lightly citrus-scented, pale yellow flowers, 3in (8cm) wide. There is one main burst of flowers, then a later scattering of blooms. For the first two years, train new shoots into a horizontal position. From then on, prune in the autumn, after flowering, nipping back the main stems if necessary and shortening sideshoots by two-thirds.

PLANT PROFILE

HEIGHT	10ft (3m)
TYPE	Climber
HARDINESS	Z5–9
FLOWERING	Summer to autumn

L   'Little White Pet'

A VIGOROUS DISPLAY OF PINK BUDS is followed by the paler flowers, which look a bit like pompons. Also known as 'White Pet', it is related to 'Félicité Perpétue' (*see page 107*) but is much smaller, making a mounded shrub for the front of the border. 'Little White Pet' is typically grown in cottage or informal gardens, and makes a colorful edging plant beside an artificial pond. Prune in late winter, removing diseased, dead, and damaged growth, and leave the old wood intact. Prune lightly to create a balanced shape; harder pruning gives fewer stems with larger flowers.

PLANT PROFILE

HEIGHT	18in (45cm)
SPREAD	22in (55cm)
TYPE	Shrub
HARDINESS	Z5–9
FLOWERING	Summer to autumn

'Louise Odier'

A WONDERFUL, OPULENT ROSE, 'Louise Odier' has large, scented, camellia-like flowers, 3⅓in (9cm) wide. In fact, they are so heavy that they bend down after the rain, but that is just part of their informal charm. 'Louise Odier' belongs to the Bourbon group and has typical tightly packed, scrunched-up petals, in this case with a dash of lilac. Growth is so vigorous that if it is grown against a wall and trained up, with no pruning, it makes a mini-climber. For a freestanding bush, prune in late winter, cutting shoots by one-half to two-thirds.

L

PLANT PROFILE

HEIGHT 6ft (2m)

SPREAD 4ft (1.2m)

TYPE Old garden rose

HARDINESS Z3–9 H9–1

FLOWERING Summer to autumn

L | LOVING MEMORY ('Korgund')

THE FLOWERS ARE SYMMETRICALLY SHAPED, and the petals are a beautiful shade of dark red. They are held on strong, upright stems and always make a good show, though the scent is not strong. A medium-high beauty, LOVING MEMORY is also good for cut flowers. Remove all unproductive stems in late winter, and prune the rest to outward-facing buds at 8–10in (20–25cm). This helps produce a vigorous, open-centered bush. Pruning harder, to just two or three buds, produces large, showy flowers.

PLANT PROFILE

HEIGHT 3½ft (1.1m)

SPREAD 2½ft (75cm)

TYPE Bush (large-flowered)

HARDINESS Z5–9

FLOWERING Summer to autumn

'Madame Alfred Carrière'

M

ONE OF THE BIG NAMES in the rose world, 'Madame Alfred Carrière' produces an overwhelming initial show followed by many more flowers. The sweetly scented blooms are cream on opening, gradually turning pinkish white. This rose can be grown on a cold, shady wall, or be pruned and grown as a massive shrub, 10ft (3m) high. Avoid pruning for the first two years, but train new shoots into a horizontal position to produce flowering sideshoots. From then on, prune in the autumn, nipping back the main stems if necessary and shortening sideshoots by two-thirds.

PLANT PROFILE

HEIGHT 15ft (5m)

TYPE Climber

HARDINESS Z5–9 H9–5

FLOWERING Summer to autumn

M | 'Madame de Sancy de Parabère'

ALTHOUGH IT FLOWERS ONLY ONCE, in early summer, this climber has large, clear pink blooms that are 5in (12cm) wide. Look closely and you will see that the outer petals are larger than the inner ones, making an attractive rosette in the center. The leaves are dark green, and the arching stems are thorn-free. Some catalogs list 'Madame de Sancy de Parabère' as a rambler. For the first two years, train new shoots horizontally to produce flowering sideshoots. From the third year, prune in autumn, trimming back the main stems if they are too long and shortening sideshoots by two-thirds.

PLANT PROFILE

HEIGHT 15ft (5m)

TYPE Climber

HARDINESS Z6–9

FLOWERING Early summer

'Madame Grégoire Staechelin'

M

A POWERHOUSE OF A CLIMBER, 'Madame Grégoire Staechelin' has one great big burst of flowers in early summer in a first-class display. The long buds open, revealing pink petals with a reddish tinge beneath, and the scent is superb. Do not snip off the fading flowers, even if you can reach them, because they are followed by attractive hips. This is a good choice for a cold, shady wall. Avoid pruning for the first two years but train new shoots horizontally. Prune in autumn from the third year by nipping back the main stems and shortening sideshoots by two-thirds.

PLANT PROFILE

HEIGHT 20ft (6m)

TYPE Climber

HARDINESS Z5–9 H9–5

FLOWERING Early summer; hips in autumn

M | 'Madame Hardy'

GIVEN A SUNNY, SHELTERED POSITION, this is one of the stars
of the white old garden roses. Beautiful and scented, 'Madame
Hardy' is a superb Damask rose. When the buds open in
midsummer for the once-only show of flowers, there is a tinge
of pink, but they quickly turn pure white with a tiny green
eye. The white stands out best against an adjacent rich red
rose. Growth is vigorous, dense, and prickly. Remove diseased,
dead, and damaged growth in late winter, and trim for a
balanced shape. Harder pruning gives fewer stems with larger
flowers, and lighter pruning the reverse.

PLANT PROFILE

HEIGHT 5ft (1.5m)

SPREAD 4ft (1.2m)

TYPE Old garden rose

HARDINESS Z4–9 H9–1

FLOWERING Summer

'Madame Isaac Pereire'

M

NOTHING SUCCEEDS LIKE EXCESS. This Bourbon rose has everything you need from an old garden rose, including a scent that is hard to beat. Each flower is a full 6in (15cm) wide, with the petals tightly packed together in a cupped shape; the late summer show is every bit as good as the first. The leaves are also large, while growth is so vigorous and arching that 'Madame Isaac Pereire' is on the verge of being a climber. If you can support the stems, even in the informality of a cottage garden, so much the better. In late winter, prune shoots by one-half to two-thirds.

PLANT PROFILE	
HEIGHT 7ft (2.2m)	
SPREAD 6ft (2m)	
TYPE Old garden rose	
HARDINESS Z6–9 H9–6	
FLOWERING Summer to autumn	

M | 'Madame Knorr'

BELONGING TO THE PORTLAND GROUP, 'Madame Knorr' has the characteristically rich scent and look of an old garden rose. The flowers are large, at 4in (10cm) wide, and the pink petals have a distinctive lilac tinge; each bloom is slightly darker in the center. There is one main flush of flowers in midsummer followed by further scatterings, but because 'Madame Knorr' is a bushy, leafy plant, it always looks attractive. Prune in late winter, cutting back stems by one-half to two-thirds. Harder pruning gives fewer stems with larger flowers, and lighter pruning more flowering stems with smaller blooms.

PLANT PROFILE

HEIGHT 4ft (1.2m)

SPREAD 3ft (1m)

TYPE Old garden rose

HARDINESS Z5–9

FLOWERING Summer to autumn

'Madame Pierre Oger'

M

AN EXCELLENT PLANT FOR A COTTAGE GARDEN, 'Madame Pierre Oger' has clusters of cupped, sweet-scented flowers. Rose experts are quick to point out the beauty of its coloring, which turns darker by a couple of shades in hot sun, while others are more concerned with possible attacks of blackspot. But for a profusion of flowers over a long period, this Bourbon rose is a very good choice. In late winter, prune by one-half to two-thirds, cutting back harder to produce fewer stems with larger flowers, and more lightly to gain more flowering stems with smaller blooms.

PLANT PROFILE	
HEIGHT	6ft (2m)
SPREAD	4ft (1.2m)
TYPE	Old garden rose
HARDINESS	Z6–9
FLOWERING	Summer to autumn

M | 'Madame Plantier'

THE EXPERTS MIGHT QUIBBLE over whether this rose is in the Alba or the Noisette group, but the key point is that it can be a large, arching shrub, studded with creamy white flowers, or a climber, spreading to 20ft (6m) across when given support. The flowers are like small pompons, flat on top, and the gray-green stems (the same color as the leaves) have few thorns. To prune for a shrub, remove only diseased, dead, and damaged growth, and trim for shape in late winter. Harder pruning results in fewer stems with larger flowers, while lighter pruning gives more stems with smaller blooms.

PLANT PROFILE

HEIGHT 6ft (2m)

SPREAD 8ft (2.5m)

TYPE Old garden rose

HARDINESS Z3–9

FLOWERING Midsummer

'Maiden's Blush'

M

SOMETIMES KNOWN AS 'GREAT MAIDEN'S BLUSH', this Alba rose has a free-and-easy look in midsummer, when there is a lovely show of pale pink, lightly scented flowers. It adds a gentle touch to cottage gardens with its blue-gray leaves, and can be incorporated in a mixed rose hedge. The French call it 'Cuisse de Nymphe', which means "thigh of the nymph," referring to its fresh, skin pink color. Remove only diseased, dead, and damaged growth, and prune lightly for shape. Harder pruning will produce fewer stems with larger flowers.

PLANT PROFILE

HEIGHT 5ft (1.5m)

SPREAD 4ft (1.2m)

TYPE Old garden rose

HARDINESS Z3–9

FLOWERING Midsummer

M | 'Maigold'

ITS EARLY-FLOWERING, HYBRID NATURE—bigger than a shrub, shorter than a typical climber—and profusion of buff-yellow flowers make 'Maigold' extremely popular. Add to that a few later flowers, the healthy, glossy foliage, and a lovely rich scent, and it is obvious why it has been a big hit since 1953. But beware of the thorny stems and note that there are no repeat flowers. There is no need to prune for the first two years, but do train new shoots into a horizontal position. From then on, prune in autumn, after flowering, nipping back the main stems and shortening sideshoots by two-thirds.

PLANT PROFILE

HEIGHT 8ft (2.5m)

TYPE Climber

HARDINESS Z5–9 H9–5

FLOWERING Early summer and autumn

MANY HAPPY RETURNS ('Harwanted')

M

IT'S NOT JUST THE NAME that has made this rose such a big hit (it won several awards in the 1980s), but also its prolific show of blush pink flowers all summer on the spreading, bushy, disease-free growth. The shiny foliage is equally attractive, giving an all-over healthy look. The autumn show of hips is a big bonus. MANY HAPPY RETURNS is worth growing toward the front of a border or even in a large tub. In late winter, cut back the main stems to 10–18in (25–45cm) above the ground, and reduce sideshoots by about one-third of their length.

PLANT PROFILE
HEIGHT 30in (75cm)
SPREAD 30in (75cm)
TYPE Bush (cluster-flowered)
HARDINESS Z6–9 H9–1
FLOWERING Summer to autumn; hips in autumn

M | 'Marchesa Boccella'

ONE OF THE PORTLAND GROUP OF ROSES, characterized by healthy growth and strong scent, 'Marchesa Boccella' is big and upright enough to make a small hedge. It has strong, thorny growth, foliage that turns grayish green, and clusters of scented, rose pink flowers. The rose sold as 'Jacques Cartier' is thought to be exactly the same. Prune stems in late winter by one-half to two-thirds. Harder pruning gives fewer stems with larger flowers, while lighter pruning gives more flowering stems with slightly smaller blooms.

PLANT PROFILE

HEIGHT	4ft (1.2m)
SPREAD	3ft (1m)
TYPE	Old garden rose
HARDINESS	Z4–9
FLOWERING	Summer to autumn

'Maréchal Niel'

M

THIS IS ONE FOR THE SPECIALIST because it is not totally hardy and the flowers do not stand up well to the rain. But give it a sunny, sheltered, modest-sized wall, and you can see why the French could not wait to get their hands on it when it was introduced in the mid–19th century. The large, high-pointed flowers are golden-yellow with a sweet scent. For the first two years, train new shoots into a horizontal position to produce flowering sideshoots. From then on, prune in autumn, after flowering, nipping back the main stems and shortening sideshoots by two-thirds.

PLANT PROFILE

HEIGHT To 15ft (5m)

TYPE Climber

HARDINESS Z7–9 H9–7

FLOWERING Summer to autumn

MARGARET MERRIL ('Harkuly')

A FIRST-RATE, PALE PINK-WHITE ROSE, it is beautifully shaped and has sweet-scented flowers of 28 petals, each bloom being 4in (10cm) wide. The flowers are perfectly set off by the crisp, dark green leaves. Though a little on the short side, MARGARET MERRIL has attractive, bushy growth and, since it was introduced in 1977, has been a big success, winning many awards, including three for fragrance. In late winter, prune back the main stems to approximately 10–18in (25–45cm) above the ground, and shorten sideshoots by one-third.

PLANT PROFILE

HEIGHT 32in (80cm)

SPREAD 24in (60cm)

TYPE Bush (cluster-flowered)

HARDINESS Z5–9 H9–5

FLOWERING Summer to autumn

'Marguerite Hilling'

M

GROWTH IS VIGOROUS AND ARCHING, and incredibly flowery. After the main burst of rose pink flowers, there are more blooms intermittently in the autumn, given good weather. 'Marguerite Hilling' also makes a very good hedge. Remove all dead, diseased, and damaged growth and prune the remaining stems quite hard in late winter to promote plenty of new, vigorous, flowering shoots.

PLANT PROFILE
HEIGHT 7ft (2.2m)
SPREAD 7ft (2.2m)
TYPE Shrub
HARDINESS Z4–9 H9–1
FLOWERING Early summer and autumn

M | MARY ROSE ('Ausmary')

WITH AN ABUNDANCE OF FLOWERS with old-world charm,
MARY ROSE is ideal for cottage gardens. It is repeat-flowering
and its blooms have a light, barely discernible scent. The
flowers will not win any prizes on the show bench, but cannot
be faulted as part of a general garden plan. Growth is twiggy,
bushy, and uneven, and perfectly disease-resistant. MARY ROSE
was introduced in 1983 to celebrate the salvage of King
Henry VIII's flagship in Hampshire, England. In late winter,
remove dead, diseased, and damaged growth, leaving the old
wood intact. Trim for shape at the same time if necessary.

PLANT PROFILE

HEIGHT 4ft (1.2m)

SPREAD 3ft (1m)

TYPE Shrub

HARDINESS Z6–9 H9–6

FLOWERING Summer to autumn

'Max Graf'

M

A VALUABLE GROUNDCOVER ROSE, 'Max Graf' (also called
R. x jacksonii 'Max Graf') produces thick, weed-suppressing
growth that roots as it extends. Let it grow freely across a bank
or tumble over a wall, but beware the thorns when weeding
nearby. The flowers have a fresh, applelike scent and appear in
one burst that lasts a long time on either side of midsummer.
Once it has taken up all the available space, prune it back in
late winter to outward-facing buds and keep an eye on it in
case it takes off again. Sideshoots can also be shortened at the
same time if necessary.

PLANT PROFILE

HEIGHT 4ft (1.2m)

SPREAD 10ft (3m) or more

TYPE Groundcover

HARDINESS Z5–9

FLOWERING Midsummer

M | 'Mermaid'

A GIANT OF A CLIMBER (even on cold, shady walls), 'Mermaid' has bright yellow, lightly scented flowers that continue through the second half of summer. It is disease-resistant and healthy, and prefers a sheltered, sunny wall. Also, it can be slow to put on growth initially, but the wait (given good conditions) is worth it. Avoid pruning for the first two years, but train new shoots into a horizontal position. From the third year, prune in autumn, after flowering, nipping back overlong main stems and shortening sideshoots by two-thirds.

PLANT PROFILE

HEIGHT To 20ft (6m)

TYPE Climber

HARDINESS Z5–9 H9–5

FLOWERING Summer to autumn

'Moonlight'

M

BUSHY AND STRONG ENOUGH to make a good hedge, 'Moonlight' has dark, glossy foliage that sets off the creamy buds. The buds gradually turn white, with a touch of yellow in the center. They appear in wonderfully impressive sprays and there is extra color from the reddish green stems. Though traditionally grown as a 4ft- (1.2m-) high shrub, it can double that figure if encouraged to spread or climb. When pruning, remove only diseased, dead, and damaged growth. A minimal late-winter pruning helps create a balanced shape, while harder pruning gives fewer stems with larger flowers.

PLANT PROFILE	
HEIGHT 4ft (1.2m)	
SPREAD 4ft (1.2m)	
TYPE Shrub	
HARDINESS Z6–9	
FLOWERING Summer to autumn	

M | 'Morning Jewel'

A USEFUL, MODEST CLIMBER, 'Morning Jewel' is happy in partial shade or full sun, and is ideal for pillars and pergola posts because it is not uncontrollably rampant. The leaves add to the show because they are healthily glossy, and the scented, bright pink flowers keep appearing all summer. It scores high points in every respect and will not let you down. It is often listed as a hybrid musk. For the first two years, train new shoots into a horizontal position to yield flowering sideshoots. From then on, prune in autumn, after flowering, trimming the main stems if necessary and sideshoots by two-thirds.

PLANT PROFILE

HEIGHT 10ft (3m)

TYPE Climber

HARDINESS Z5–9 H9–1

FLOWERING Summer to autumn

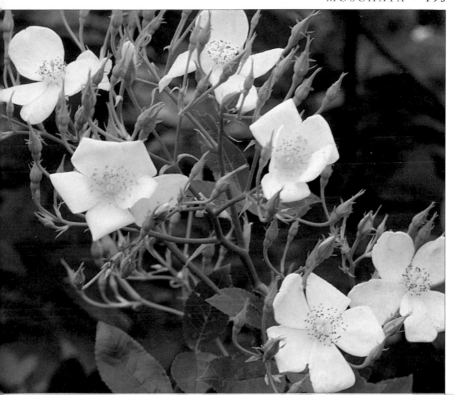

moschata Musk rose

M

SOMETIMES CALLED A SMALL CLIMBER (or rambler), or tall shrub, the most important thing about this rose is that the flowers do not appear until late summer, and that is why it is grown. They bloom in a beautiful show of open, scented, creamy white sprays, with purplish green leaves, which carries on into autumn. *R. moschata* was rediscovered in the early 1960s (having first appeared in the 16th century), and adds a relaxed touch in cottage gardens. Leave the fading flowers uncut and you will get plenty of orange-red hips. Minimal pruning is required.

PLANT PROFILE

HEIGHT To 10ft (3m)

SPREAD To 10ft (3m)

TYPE Wild

HARDINESS Z7–9

FLOWERING Late summer to autumn; hips in autumn

M | MOUNTBATTEN ('Harmantelle')

VIGOROUS, TALL, AND SHRUBBY with a good covering of large, dark green leaves, MOUNTBATTEN is not typical of the cluster-flowered bush roses. Its first batch of flowers is very impressive—they are about 4in (10cm) wide and cupped, on long stems—with many more after, as you would expect from a rose that has received several awards and medals. A good choice for a novice gardener. In late winter, cut back the main stems to 10–18in (25–45cm) long, and reduce the sideshoots by two-thirds of their length.

PLANT PROFILE

HEIGHT	4ft (1.2m)
SPREAD	30in (75cm)
TYPE	Bush (cluster-flowered)
HARDINESS	Z5–9 H9–5
FLOWERING	Summer to autumn

moyesii 'Geranium'

M

THIS ROSE HAS BRIGHT, CHERRY RED FLOWERS followed by superb, large red hips in late summer, and lovely, bright green leaves. Its parent, *R. moyesii*, is a giant, at 12ft (4m) high and 10ft (3m) wide, with scarlet flowers and red hips, so unless you have a huge garden, *R. moyesii* 'Geranium' is the one to go for. Remove only diseased, dead, and damaged growth in late winter, and give a general trim for a balanced shape.

PLANT PROFILE
HEIGHT 8ft (2.5m)
SPREAD 5ft (1.5m)
TYPE Shrub
HARDINESS Z4–9 H9–1
FLOWERING Summer; hips in late summer

M | 'Mrs. John Laing'

THE ROUNDED, CUPPED FLOWERS contain tightly packed petals, and have a lovely, strong scent. The color is more silvery pink with a hint of lilac than plain pink, giving an added attraction, while the virtually thorn-free stems make it an easy rose to weed around. It grows well, even in poor soil, and adds a gentle hue to pastel schemes. In formal gardens, prune shoots by one-half to two-thirds in late winter. In less formal and cottage gardens, remove only diseased, dead, and damaged growth, and give a light overall pruning for shape.

PLANT PROFILE

HEIGHT 3ft (1m)

SPREAD 30in (75cm)

TYPE Old garden rose

HARDINESS Z5–9 H9–5

FLOWERING Summer to autumn

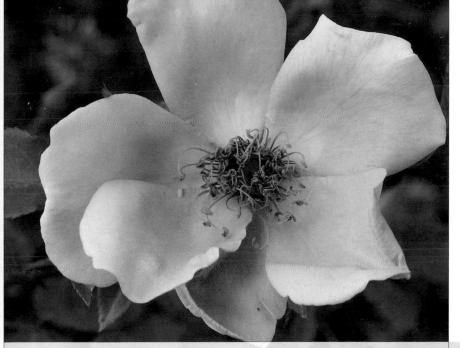

'Mrs. Oakley Fisher'

M

SINCE BEING INTRODUCED IN 1921, 'Mrs. Oakley Fisher' has been highly regarded by rose experts for its slightly unusual, highly scented flowers. The flowers are flat and 3in (8cm) wide, combining orange and yellow on spindly stems with sparse, bronze-green foliage. The flower color eventually fades to pale buff yellow. In late winter, remove all unproductive stems, and prune the remainder hard to outward-facing buds at 8–10in (20–25cm) above ground. This helps remove crisscrossing shoots in the center of the bush. For larger, showier flowers, prune harder, leaving just two or three buds.

PLANT PROFILE

HEIGHT	To 3ft (1m)
SPREAD	To 3ft (1m)
TYPE	Bush (large-flowered)
HARDINESS	Z5–9
FLOWERING	Summer to autumn

M | *mulliganii*

A MASSIVE, RAMPANT ROSE, *R. mulliganii* is an incredibly vigorous wild rambler and needs careful siting. A strong host tree is needed to support its growth, which hangs on with hooked thorns. There is a profusion of small flower clusters, plus a fruity scent and glossy, dark green leaves. Added color comes from the reddish new shoots, the creamy buds, and the orange-red hips. The overall impact is hugely impressive. In late summer, for the first two years, prune sideshoots by 3in (8cm) to a strong new shoot. From then on, prune up to one-third of the oldest main stems to ground level.

PLANT PROFILE

HEIGHT To 20ft (6m)

TYPE Rambler

HARDINESS Z5–9

FLOWERING Midsummer; hips in autumn

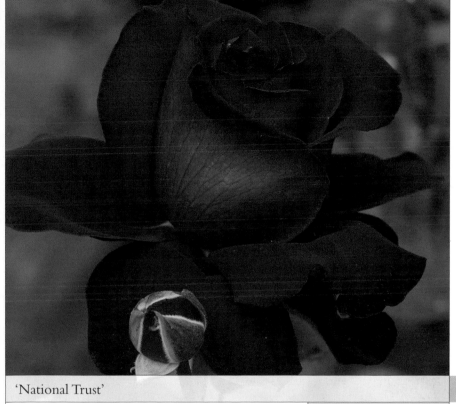

'National Trust'

WITH EXQUISITE FLOWERS that withstand bad weather and sit smartly upright on strong stems against dark green leaves, this rose is a winner, except for its lack of scent. Its small size means it is easy to find room for at the front of a border, or in a mixed rose garden. It makes good gift for anyone who thinks such roses do not belong in contemporary gardens. Prune in late winter, removing unproductive stems, and cut back the remainder hard to outward-facing buds 8–10in (20–25cm) above the ground. For large, showy flowers, prune harder, leaving just two or three buds.

PLANT PROFILE	
HEIGHT 24in (60cm)	
SPREAD 24in (60cm)	
TYPE Bush (large-flowered)	
HARDINESS Z5–9	
FLOWERING Summer to autumn	

N '**Nevada**'

ON A HOT, SUNNY DAY before midsummer, 'Nevada' is absolutely packed with flowers and there are few roses to rival it. Each flower is about 4in (10cm) wide and the stems, before they are obscured, are reddish brown. After the main burst of flowers, there are more blooms, intermittently, in the autumn, given good weather. 'Nevada' also makes a very good hedge. Prune by removing only diseased, dead, and damaged growth, leaving the old wood intact. Give a trim in late winter to help produce a balanced shape; harder pruning gives fewer stems with larger flowers.

PLANT PROFILE

HEIGHT 7ft (2.2m)

SPREAD 7ft (2.2m)

TYPE Shrub

HARDINESS Z4–9 H9–1

FLOWERING Early summer and sparsely in autumn

'New Dawn'

A BIG HIT when it was introduced in 1930, 'New Dawn' remains a big seller for three reasons: the pale, pearl pink, scented flowers keep opening in clusters from midsummer after the initial burst, the growth is reasonably restrained, and the leaves are attractively glossy. Also, it can be trained into trees, grown as a large bush, or incorporated in a hedge. It even grows on cold, shady walls. In the first two years, train new shoots into a horizontal position. From then on, prune in the autumn, after flowering, nipping back any overlong main stems and shortening sideshoots by two-thirds.

PLANT PROFILE

HEIGHT 10ft (3m)

TYPE Climber

HARDINESS Z5–9 H9–5

FLOWERING Summer to autumn

N | NICE DAY ('Chewsea')

A MINIATURE CLIMBER, this is just what you need where space is extremely limited. The small, scented flowers (which are shaped like a rosette) are a lovely mix of salmon, orange, and pink, and the buds keep opening in clusters over the summer months. If you try to prune them to restrict height, the plants respond by putting up more climbing shoots from the base, where you don't want them, making the rose bushier. In other words, when it comes to pruning, don't.

PLANT PROFILE

HEIGHT 6ft (2m)

TYPE Climber

HARDINESS Z4–9

FLOWERING Summer

'Noisette Carnée'

SOMETIMES CALLED 'BLUSH NOISETTE', this is a dual–purpose Noisette rose. It can either be trained against a sunny, sheltered wall, growing to 12ft (4m), or be allowed to mound at the back of a border, where it makes a large shrub 6ft (2m) high. It may not be an all-time favorite, but it does have dark pink buds, repeat-flowers well, and, with its old-fashioned look, is ideal for the cottage garden. For a climber, train new shoots horizontally for the first two years. Then prune in autumn, trimming the main stems, and shortening sideshoots by two-thirds. For a shrub, remove dead, diseased, and damaged wood.

PLANT PROFILE

HEIGHT 6–12ft (2–4m)

TYPE Climber

HARDINESS Z6–9

FLOWERING Summer to autumn

N NORFOLK ('Poulfolk')

COVERING A SMALL AREA with scented, yellow flowers, this is not exactly the widest-spreading groundcover rose available, but with its dense growth, it keeps down weeds, and does the job very well. The leaves are healthy, glossy green, which compensates for the sporadic show of flowers after the main burst. NORFOLK can also be grown in tubs and large pots. Minimal pruning is required, but if growth is getting too rampant, cut back to an outward-facing bud in late winter. Shorten sideshoots at the same time if necessary.

PLANT PROFILE

HEIGHT 30in (75cm)

SPREAD 3ft (1m)

TYPE Groundcover

HARDINESS Z5–9

FLOWERING Summer

'Nozomi'

N

A GROUNDCOVER ROSE with a difference, 'Nozomi' can also be trained and encouraged to grow up a post on an arbor, or a short pillar, to a height of about 5ft (1.5m). Either way, it makes trailing growth covered by glossy, dark green leaves and clusters of barely scented, small, pale pink-white flowers in summer. Because it flowers on the previous year's wood, prune it lightly or you will remove all this year's flower buds and end up with a shapely plant but hardly any flowers.

PLANT PROFILE

HEIGHT	18in (45cm)
SPREAD	4ft (1.2m)
TYPE	Groundcover
HARDINESS	Z5–9 H9–5
FLOWERING	Summer

N | *nutkana* 'Plena'

IN SOME REFERENCE BOOKS this rose goes under its old name of *R. californica* 'Plena'. You are likely to find it only in specialist nurseries, which is a shame because it is a terrific, leafy shrub. The sprays of rich pink flowers, with yellow stamens in the center, appear on the arching, reddish brown wood that has sharp gray thorns. It grows to quite a size, and looks best in cottage gardens and hedges. To create a large shrub, remove only diseased, dead, and damaged growth. Harder pruning gives fewer stems with larger flowers, and lighter pruning more stems but smaller blooms.

PLANT PROFILE

HEIGHT 5–8ft (1.5–2.5m)

SPREAD 4–6ft (1.2–2m)

TYPE Wild

HARDINESS Z3–9

FLOWERING Midsummer

x *odorata* 'Mutabilis'

THIS SPECTACULAR CHINA ROSE needs a sunny, sheltered position. In mild weather it starts flowering in late spring, and after its main flower burst in early summer, new buds keep appearing, never with quite the same intensity, but always adding plenty of color. Growth is twiggy and open, and long, lax stems may need support. Even before it starts flowering, it is beautifully colored with plum-red new stems and fluttering leaves. The flowers open copper-yellow, changing to pink, then copper-crimson before falling. Against a wall, it will climb to 10ft (3m). Give a light late-winter trim for shape.

PLANT PROFILE	
HEIGHT 6ft (2m)	
SPREAD 6ft (2m)	
TYPE Old garden rose	
HARDINESS Z7–9 H9–7	
FLOWERING Late spring to autumn	

O | x *odorata* 'Viridiflora' Green rose

A BIZARRE CHINA ROSE that you will not find in the average garden, it has promising bluish green buds that open to reveal clusters of small green petals, resembling leaves, which soon acquire a purplish brown color. It is more likely to elicit a "What's that?" than a "Where can I get one?" but if you crave something very different, this is one to try. In late winter, prune shoots by one-half to two-thirds. The harder you prune, the fewer the stems and the larger the flowers, while lighter pruning gives more stems with smaller blooms.

PLANT PROFILE	
HEIGHT 30in (75cm)	
SPREAD 30in (75cm)	
TYPE Old garden rose	
HARDINESS Z6–9	
FLOWERING Summer to autumn	

ORANGES AND LEMONS ('Macoranlem')

O

IN THE RIGHT SCHEME, the upright ORANGES AND LEMONS is a big plus. The flowers are a strange mishmash of an orange-yellow background and scarlet (fading to pinkish red) stripes, speckles, and blotches. The first reaction is either a definite "yes" or a "not in my garden." Its glossy, dark green leaves are nicely colored with a red tinge when they are young. In late winter, cut back the main stems to 10–18in (25–45cm) above the ground, and shorten sideshoots by about one-third.

PLANT PROFILE	
HEIGHT 32in (80cm)	
SPREAD 24in (60cm)	
TYPE Bush (cluster-flowered)	
HARDINESS Z5–9	
FLOWERING Summer to autumn	

P

PARTRIDGE ('Korweirim')

THIS IS ONE OF THE WIDEST-SPREADING groundcover roses, and it definitely needs a lot of space. For that reason it can also be grown over banks and tumbling over a wall, and it makes nice, rampant edging along the side of an artificial pond. Unlike many groundcover roses, PARTRIDGE also has a strong scent. Minimal pruning is required, but if growth is getting too rampant, cut it back to an outward-facing bud in late winter. Sideshoots can also be shortened then if necessary. Don't expect to keep it small, though.

PLANT PROFILE

HEIGHT 30in (75cm)

SPREAD 10ft (3m)

TYPE Groundcover

HARDINESS Z6–9

FLOWERING Mid- and late summer

'Paul Neyron'

P

THE BEST REASONS FOR GROWING this Hybrid Perpetual rose
are the enormous, 6in- (15cm-) wide flowers, with ruffled,
lilac-tinged, deep pink petals (without a strong scent to
match). From a distance they look like peonies and, while
some dislike their extravagance, 'Paul Neyron' does provide
wonderful cut flowers and a blowsy touch for cottage gardens.
Growth is vigorous and upright. In formal gardens, prune
shoots by one-half to two-thirds in late winter. In less formal
and cottage gardens, remove only diseased, dead, and damaged
growth, and give a light overall pruning for shape.

PLANT PROFILE	
HEIGHT 5ft (1.5m)	
SPREAD 4ft (1.2m)	
TYPE Old garden rose	
HARDINESS Z5–9	
FLOWERING Summer to autumn	

PAUL SHIRVILLE ('Harqueterwife')

AN EXQUISITE ROSE, the color is hard to pin down and is much more than plain pink; there are hints of rosy salmon, and possibly peach. It is worth a place toward the front of a pastel border, while the flowers perk up cut-flower displays. The first batch of scented flowers have high centers, though subsequent blooms might not be quite as good. In late winter, remove unproductive stems and prune the rest to outward-facing buds at 8–10in (20–25cm). This helps remove crisscrossing shoots in the center of the bush. For large, showy flowers, prune harder, to two or three buds.

PLANT PROFILE

HEIGHT 3ft (1m)

SPREAD 30in (75cm)

TYPE Bush (large-flowered)

HARDINESS Z5–9 H9–5

FLOWERING Summer to autumn

'Paul's Himalayan Musk'

P

THE LONG, THIN STEMS need to be trained up into a tree, where they shoot out arching, prickly growth. Then, just before midsummer, hundreds of sprays of tiny buds appear. Each flower is small and insignificant, but when every bud is open the tree turns into a fantastic whoosh of pale pink. There is only one show of flowers, but it is terrific. In late summer, for the first two years, prune sideshoots by 3in (8cm) to a strong new shoot. From the third year, prune up to one-third of the oldest main stems to ground level.

PLANT PROFILE

HEIGHT 30ft (10m)

TYPE Rambler

HARDINESS Z6–9 H9–6

FLOWERING Midsummer

P

'Paul's Lemon Pillar'

NOT THE BIGGEST CLIMBER, but the once-only show of flowers does come just before midsummer, with a gentle citrus scent. The 5in- (12cm-) wide, high-pointed flowers are beautifully shaped, on stiff, upright stems that can be trained around a pillar or the post of a pergola. Provide adjacent climbers to flower before and afterward, and you have a first-rate show. For the first two years, train new shoots into a horizontal position to produce flowering sideshoots. Then prune regularly in the autumn, nipping back the main stems if necessary and shortening sideshoots by two-thirds.

PLANT PROFILE

HEIGHT	12ft (4m)
TYPE	Climber
HARDINESS	Z5–9 H9–5
FLOWERING	Summer

'Paul's Scarlet Climber'

THE BREAKING OPEN OF THE BUDS and the great show of scarlet flowers is a good way to start summer. If it is the only climbing rose in the garden, it has relatively little to offer, since it is not scented, and there is just one show of flowers. But in combination with others (flowering before and after), it is a good, striking choice. It is sometimes listed in catalogs as a rambler. Avoid pruning for the first two years, but train new shoots into a horizontal position for flowering sideshoots. Prune in the autumn from the third year, nipping back overlong main stems and shortening sideshoots by two-thirds.

PLANT PROFILE

HEIGHT 10ft (3m)

TYPE Climber

HARDINESS Z5–9

FLOWERING Early summer

P | PEACE ('Madame A. Meilland')

THE PINK-TINGED, YELLOW PEACE was once one of the biggest names in the rose world. There has been a bit of a backlash due to overkill and snobbery, but it remains a fine choice. Growth is shrubby and vigorous, with glossy, dark green foliage, and the flowers are heavy and 6in (15cm) across but lack scent. It is a good choice for the beginner, requiring little pruning. In late winter, remove unproductive stems, and prune the rest to outward-facing buds at 8–10in (20–25cm). This helps remove crossing shoots in the center. For large, showy flowers, prune harder, to just two or three buds.

PLANT PROFILE	
HEIGHT 4ft (1.2m)	
SPREAD 3ft (1m)	
TYPE Bush (large-flowered)	
HARDINESS Z5–9 H9–5	
FLOWERING Summer to autumn	

PEARL DRIFT ('Leggab')

P

EQUALLY GOOD AS A SHRUB or a low, dense hedge, this rose has a good covering of large, glossy, dark green leaves. The flowers are on the cottage-garden side, being flat and open with yellow stamens, rather than sophisticated and shapely, and they repeat-flower over summer. PEARL DRIFT has an easygoing, relaxed feel. Some rose growers detect a hint of pink in the flowers, but if so, it is very subtle. Remove only diseased, dead, and damaged growth when pruning. A minimal late-winter pruning yields a balanced shape. Harder pruning gives fewer stems with larger flowers, and lighter pruning the reverse.

PLANT PROFILE	
HEIGHT 3ft (1m)	
SPREAD 4ft (1.2m)	
TYPE Shrub	
HARDINESS Z5–9 H9–5	
FLOWERING Summer to autumn	

P

'Penelope'

WONDERFUL SPRAYS OF SALMON-PINK BUDS and creamy pink flowers last over the summer, more creamy than pink in full sun, followed by hips. Initially green, the hips soon turn reddish pink. Prune it and it stays small, but untouched it will reach 6ft (2m) tall and wide. Rose experts get carried away when describing 'Penelope', and there is no doubt that the unpruned version makes a strong impression. Remove only diseased, dead, and damaged growth, and leave the old wood. A minimal pruning in late winter yields a balanced shape. If required, harder pruning gives fewer stems with larger flowers.

PLANT PROFILE

HEIGHT 3½ft (1.1m)

SPREAD 3½ft (1.1m)

TYPE Shrub

HARDINESS Z6–9 H9–6

FLOWERING Summer to autumn; hips in autumn

PENNY LANE ('Hardwell')

IN 1998 IT WAS VOTED ROSE OF THE YEAR in the UK, the first climber to gain that honor. PENNY LANE combines the charm of an old garden rose with a continuous supply of flowers over summer on stiff stems with healthy, dark green leaves. The light honey-colored flowers slowly turn pale pink. It is ideal in cottage gardens, growing up a pergola or over an arch, and adds a calming touch to brighter colors. In the first two years, train new shoots horizontally. From the third year, prune in the autumn, nipping back overlong main stems, and shortening sideshoots by two-thirds.

PLANT PROFILE	
HEIGHT	12ft (4m)
TYPE	Climber
HARDINESS	Z5–9
FLOWERING	Summer

P

'Perle d'Or'

SCORING HIGH POINTS for its lovely scent, this China rose also has a covering of yellowish orange, urn-shaped buds that open to reveal pale apricot-colored flowers, which turn creamy with age, set against dark green leaves. Growth is twiggy and spindly. The translation of the name means "golden pearl," which reflects the plant raiser's aim rather than the reality. In late winter, prune shoots by one-half to two-thirds, pruning harder for fewer stems with larger flowers, and more lightly for more flowering stems with slightly smaller blooms.

PLANT PROFILE

HEIGHT	To 4ft (1.2m)
SPREAD	3ft (1m)
TYPE	Old garden rose
HARDINESS	Z4–11 H12–1
FLOWERING	Summer to autumn

PHEASANT ('Kordapt')

P

ONE OF THE MOST IMPRESSIVE groundcover roses, it has an immense spread and a repeat show of scented flowers, but do not think about growing it unless you have enough space. Good sites include a bank, or tumbling over a wall. The repeat-flowering is definitely a bonus, but the eventual size might well put many people off: this is a giant. Minimal pruning is needed, but if shoots are getting too rampant, cut them back to outward-facing buds in late winter, and shorten sideshoots. Do not hope to restrain it significantly by pruning.

PLANT PROFILE

HEIGHT 20in (50cm)

SPREAD 10ft (3m)

TYPE Groundcover

HARDINESS Z5–9

FLOWERING Summer

'Phyllis Bide'

OF THE CLIMBERS AND RAMBLERS that reach 8ft (2.5m) high, this might not have the strongest, richest color (being yellow with a tinge of pale pink), but it probably gives the most immense covering with sprays of flowers. And that sweet-scented display keeps on, all summer, until the autumn, with small and dainty flowers and leaves. It is very impressive against walls and over pergolas. For the first two years, avoid pruning, but train sideshoots horizontally. From then on, prune in the autumn, cutting back overlong main stems and shortening sideshoots by about two-thirds.

PLANT PROFILE	
HEIGHT 8ft (2.5m)	
TYPE Climber	
HARDINESS Z6–9	
FLOWERING Summer to autumn	

PICCADILLY ('Macar')

P

ONE OF THE BEST of the twin-colored roses, PICCADILLY is red on top and yellow underneath, and what sounds like a gaudy combination is actually a blended merging of the two colors. The faintly scented flowers are set against the reddish green foliage, giving a high-quality rose that is hard to fault. In late winter, remove all unproductive stems, and prune hard to outward-facing buds, leaving 8–10in (20–25cm) of stem above the ground. This helps remove crossing shoots in the center of the bush. For large, showy flowers, prune harder, to just two or three buds.

PLANT PROFILE

HEIGHT 32in (80cm)

SPREAD 24in (60cm)

TYPE Bush (large-flowered)

HARDINESS Z5–9 H9–5

FLOWERING Summer to autumn

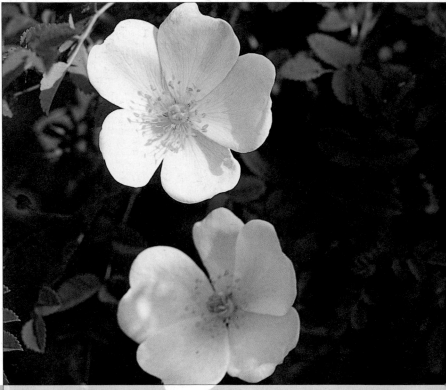

P | *pimpinellifolia* 'Dunwich Rose'

TWO OF THESE ROSES, framing a large pot or special feature, add an effective cottage-garden touch. Growth is small, mounding, and free, with arching, prickly, wiry stems covered at the start of summer with pale lemon flowers followed by black hips. In the wild it grows on sandy coastal sites, sending plenty of new shoots out of the ground. If they spread too far, pull them off. The parent *R. pimpinellifolia* has white flowers. When pruning in late winter, remove only diseased, dead, and damaged growth, and trim to produce a balanced shape.

PLANT PROFILE

HEIGHT 26in (65cm)

SPREAD 4ft (1.2m)

TYPE Shrub

HARDINESS Z3–9

FLOWERING Early summer; hips in autumn

PINK BELLS ('Poulbells')

THE BELLS SERIES OFFERS SHORT, VERTICAL GROWTH and
wide, outward-spreading stems with glossy foliage and sprays
of smallish, bright pink flowers. They appear in mid- and late
summer, when the dense growth keeps down weeds. PINK
BELLS cannot be packed into a small space, and is far too big
for most borders. Use it on a spare patch of ground where the
soil is not necessarily first-rate. Minimal pruning is required,
but if growth is too rampant, cut shoots back to outward-
facing buds in late winter. Sideshoots can also be shortened
then, but pruning will not restrain its vigorous spread.

P

PLANT PROFILE

HEIGHT 30in (75cm)

SPREAD 5ft (1.5m)

TYPE Groundcover

HARDINESS Z5–9 H9–5

FLOWERING Summer

P   'Pink Grootendorst'

NOT QUITE AS VIGOROUS AND LARGE as its crimson-red
parent, 'F. J. Grootendorst', this rose has clusters of rose pink
blooms, which last well as cut flowers. It reliably flowers over
summer, is disease-free, has upright, dense growth, and, with
its coarse, dark green leaves, makes a perfectly decent cottage-
garden hedge. A few specialist nurseries sell 'White
Grootendorst', and both are usually listed as Rugosa roses in
catalogs. In late winter, prune shoots by one-half to two-
thirds; harder pruning gives fewer stems with larger flowers,
and lighter pruning more stems with smaller blooms.

PLANT PROFILE

HEIGHT 4½ft (1.3m)

SPREAD 3½ft (1.1m)

TYPE Shrub

HARDINESS Z3–9 H9–1

FLOWERING Summer to autumn

'Pink Perpétué'

IT MIGHT BE RESTRAINED IN HEIGHT, but not when it comes to repeat-flowering—the faintly scented pink blooms (richer pink beneath) keep appearing as late as autumn. Each flower is 3in (8cm) wide. Growth is easily trained up arches, pergolas, or even fences, where you can take advantage of its wide-spreading habit. The leaves are leathery and dark green. For the first two years, train new shoots into a horizontal position. From then on, prune in the autumn, after flowering, nipping back the main stems if they are too long and shortening sideshoots by two-thirds.

PLANT PROFILE	
HEIGHT To 10ft (3m)	
TYPE Climber	
HARDINESS Z5–9 H9–5	
FLOWERING Summer to autumn	

P | POLAR STAR ('Tanlarpost')

SOMETIMES KNOWN AS 'POLAR STERN', the UK Rose of the Year in 1985 has a big garden presence. The large, white, barely scented flowers are nearly 5in (12cm) wide, abundant, and do not collapse in the rain. The growth stands tall and upright. Some might find 'Polar Star' a bit too obvious, but it is clearly very popular. In late winter, remove the unproductive stems and prune hard to outward-facing buds at 8–10in (20–25cm) from the ground. Choosing an outward-facing bud helps deter crossing shoots in the center. For large, showy flowers, prune harder, to two or three buds.

PLANT PROFILE

HEIGHT 3ft (1m)

SPREAD 28in (70cm)

TYPE Bush (large-flowered)

HARDINESS Z5–9

FLOWERING Summer to autumn

Pot o' Gold ('Dicdivine')

The buds suggest high–centered flowers but they actually end up attractively cupped. The fragrant, medium-sized, golden yellow flowers appear in large numbers (alone or in clusters) in summer and into autumn, withstanding rain and diseases. Pot o' Gold rarely disappoints in the border (especially in cottage gardens, where flower profusion is more important than perfectly shaped blooms), putting on vigorous, spreading growth. Prune in late winter, removing all unproductive stems, and cutting the rest to outward-facing buds at 8–10in (20–25cm). For large flowers, prune harder, to two or three buds.

P

PLANT PROFILE	
HEIGHT	30in (75cm)
SPREAD	24in (60cm)
TYPE	Bush (large-flowered)
HARDINESS	Z5–9 H9–5
FLOWERING	Summer to autumn

P | 'Président de Sèze'

THIS MAKES A SPECIAL SIGHT for two reasons. First, the flowers have a wonderful two-tone color, being rich magenta-crimson in the center and lilac around the edges, which is even more surprising given that the buds are pink. Second, growth is strong with large leaves, making an attractive, open shape. A row of these Gallica roses makes a colorful summer divide, but they are not dense enough to make a conventional hedge. Remove only diseased, dead, and damaged growth, and give a light late-winter pruning for a balanced shape. Harder pruning gives fewer stems with larger flowers.

PLANT PROFILE

HEIGHT	4ft (1.2m)
SPREAD	4ft (1.2m)
TYPE	Old garden rose
HARDINESS	Z3–9 H9–1
FLOWERING	Summer

PRETTY POLLY ('Meitonje')

PRETTY POLLY IS ONE OF THE BEST of its kind. It is compact, bushy, and very vigorous, putting out a huge number of small flowers over summer. It is just right for a pot, or for edging the length of a path or the sides of a patio. The healthy-looking leaves are dark green. It may be hard to find in garden centers but is sold by specialist nurseries, sometimes being listed as a slightly taller patio rose. In late winter, select the strongest shoots and remove all other growth. Cut the shoots back by approximately one-third to one-half. This regimen forces up plenty of new, vigorous growth.

PLANT PROFILE

HEIGHT 16in (40cm)

SPREAD 18in (45cm)

TYPE Bush (cluster-flowered, miniature)

HARDINESS Z5–9

FLOWERING Summer to autumn

P

'Prima Ballerina'

THE LOVELY, RICH SCENT, beautiful shade of pink, and clearly visible, shapely flowers that stand up on strong necks compensate for the likelihood of mildew. 'Prima Ballerina' can be grown in groups of three or so in a mixed border, or as one of the highlights in a pastel scheme. The pink petals are more rich and warm than pale and slight. Prune in late winter, removing all unproductive stems, and cut the rest hard to outward-facing buds at 8–10in (20–25cm). This helps remove crisscrossing shoots in the center. For large, showy flowers, prune harder, leaving just two or three buds.

PLANT PROFILE

HEIGHT 3ft (1m)

SPREAD 24in (60cm)

TYPE Bush (large-flowered)

HARDINESS Z5–9

FLOWERING Summer to autumn

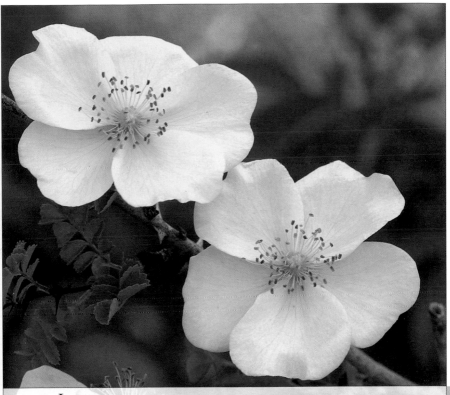

primula Incense rose

P

THE SMELL (NOT QUITE LIKE INCENSE) actually comes from the young leaves, which have a slight gray tinge. The young stems are more colorful, being reddish brown, while the flowers, emerging at the end of spring, tend to be pale primrose. They are followed by brownish maroon hips. *R. primula* is a lovely, carefree sight with its almost arching, graceful stems and unobtrusive flowers. It makes a good start to the summer in cottage gardens. Remove only diseased, dead, and damaged growth. A minimal late-winter pruning also helps produce a more balanced shape, if required.

PLANT PROFILE	
HEIGHT To 10ft (3m)	
SPREAD 6ft (2m)	
TYPE Wild	
HARDINESS Z5–9 H9–5	
FLOWERING Late spring; hips in autumn	

P | 'Pristine'

ON THE TALL AND THIN SIDE, 'Pristine' has healthy, upright growth with large, dark green leaves and stands out in the border. It won a Royal National Rose Society medal for fragrance in 1973. The 5in- (12cm-) wide, shapely flowers are high-centered and well worth including in cut-flower displays. In the garden, the petals retain their pink color without any fading. In late winter, remove unproductive stems, and prune to outward-facing buds at 8–10in (20–25cm). For large, showy flowers, prune harder, to just two or three buds. You are aiming for an open-centered bush shape, with no crossing shoots.

PLANT PROFILE

HEIGHT 4ft (1.2m)

SPREAD 30in (75cm)

TYPE Bush (large-flowered)

HARDINESS Z5–9

FLOWERING Summer to autumn

'Prosperity'

P

A LARGE SHRUB, 'Prosperity' has a profusion of light pink buds opening to creamy white, nicely scented flowers, each 2in (5cm) wide. The dark green leaves provide a good background. It was introduced in 1919, and remains a high-class plant. 'Prosperity', like other hybrid musks with a similar multitude of smallish flowers, can be grown in large borders, though it can also be trained up against a wall. Remove diseased, dead, and damaged growth and give a minimal late-winter trim for a balanced shape. Harder pruning gives fewer stems with larger flowers, and lighter pruning more stems with smaller blooms.

PLANT PROFILE

HEIGHT 6ft (2m)

SPREAD 4ft (1.2m)

TYPE Shrub

HARDINESS Z6–9

FLOWERING Summer to autumn

Q | QUEEN MOTHER ('Korquemu')

ON THE BORDERLINE between a patio and a slightly shorter miniature rose, QUEEN MOTHER has beautiful, soft pink flowers. They appear in large numbers on spreading, bushy growth, set against the glossy green foliage. It looks equally attractive in pots or the garden, where it can be used to edge paths or fill gaps. In late winter, remove all growth apart from the strongest shoots, and cut them back by one-third to one-half. This regimen forces up plenty of new, vigorous growth.

PLANT PROFILE

HEIGHT 16in (40cm)

SPREAD 24in (60cm)

TYPE Bush (cluster-flowered, patio)

HARDINESS Z5–9

FLOWERING Summer to autumn

'Rambling Rector'

IT PRODUCES A FANTASTIC SHOW of vigorous, arching stems with sweetly scented, small, open flowers with a yellow center, followed by red hips. Grow it up into a substantial tree and its midsummer show will burst through the canopy in a mass of sprays. The prolific growth can easily cover an old shed or be incorporated into a hedgerow where the small thorns lock on to the host plant. In late summer, for the first two years, prune sideshoots by 3in (8cm) to a strong new shoot. From the third year, prune at most one-third of the oldest main stems back to ground level.

PLANT PROFILE

HEIGHT 20ft (6m)

TYPE Rambler

HARDINESS Z5–9 H9–5

FLOWERING Summer; hips in autumn

R | 'Raubritter'

BECAUSE IT GROWS TWICE AS WIDE as it does tall, some catalogs list 'Raubritter' as a groundcover rose. It makes a large, sprawling, bushy mound with crisscrossing branches covered in dark green leaves and light pink flowers in a one-time midsummer display. It will certainly keep down weeds, but can also be grown to cover a bank or trail over a wall. Remove only diseased, dead, and damaged growth. A minimal late-winter pruning also helps produce a balanced shape and more flowering stems with smaller blooms, while harder pruning gives fewer stems with larger flowers.

PLANT PROFILE

HEIGHT 3ft (1m)

SPREAD 6ft (2m)

TYPE Shrub

HARDINESS Z5–9

FLOWERING Midsummer

RED BLANKET ('Intercell')

R

HIGHLY EFFECTIVE AS GROUNDCOVER, 'Red Blanket' produces spreading, bushy growth covered in a mass of dark green leaves. The big features of the flowers are that the red pales to white in the center, and that the blooms appear in clusters over a long period through summer. The possibility of blackspot should not put you off. Little pruning is needed, but if the growth is getting too rampant, cut it back to an outward-facing bud in late winter. Sideshoots can also be shortened at the same time if necessary.

PLANT PROFILE

HEIGHT 30in (75cm)

SPREAD 4ft (1.2m)

TYPE Groundcover

HARDINESS Z5–9

FLOWERING Summer to autumn

R

'Reine des Violettes'

CLOSE TO AN OLD GARDEN ROSE in terms of flower shape and color, 'Reine des Violettes' has the extra advantage of flowering well through summer into autumn, on virtually thorn-free stems. The flowers are purple on opening before turning slightly paler and then lilac. It was introduced in 1860 and experts still put this Hybrid Perpetual high on their list of must-have roses. Pamper it with deep, rich soil. In formal gardens, prune shoots by one-half to two-thirds in late winter. In less formal and cottage gardens, remove only diseased, dead, and damaged growth, and give a light overall pruning for shape.

PLANT PROFILE

HEIGHT 5ft (1.5m)

SPREAD 4ft (1.2m)

TYPE Old garden rose

HARDINESS Z5–9 H9–5

FLOWERING Summer to autumn

'Reine Victoria'

NAMED IN HONOR OF QUEEN VICTORIA in 1872, this Bourbon rose is nothing like her forbidding, gray, huffy image. The flowers are beautifully cupped and rounded with 40 petals, rich pink with a hint of mauve, on top of strong, erect, bushy growth. It exudes old-world charm, and is well worth including in a collection of old garden roses or at the back of a cottage-garden border. In late winter, prune shoots by one-half to two-thirds. Harder pruning gives fewer stems with larger flowers, and lighter pruning more flowering stems with smaller blooms.

PLANT PROFILE

HEIGHT 6ft (2m)

SPREAD 4ft (1.2m)

TYPE Old garden rose

HARDINESS Z6–9 H9–6

FLOWERING Summer to autumn

R | REMEMBER ME ('Cocdestin')

OF ALL THE COPPER-COLORED ROSES, this is one of the darkest. The flowers are nearly 4in (10cm) wide, appearing singly or in sprays on stiff, bushy growth. The leaves are glossy, dark green, creating an effective contrast. REMEMBER ME makes a nice addition to hothouse borders, combining well with reds and yellows, and keeps flowering into autumn. In late winter, remove all unproductive stems, and prune the rest hard to outward-facing buds at 8–10in (20–25cm). This helps remove crisscrossing shoots in the center of the bush. For large, showy flowers, prune to just two or three buds.

PLANT PROFILE

HEIGHT 3ft (1m)

SPREAD 24in (60cm)

TYPE Bush (large-flowered)

HARDINESS Z5–9 H9–5

FLOWERING Summer to autumn

ROBIN REDBREAST ('Interrob')

R

A MODEST GROUNDCOVER ROSE compared to some of the vigorous wide-spreaders, ROBIN REDBREAST makes dense, bushy, thorny growth. The scentless, dark red flowers are small and open with a white eye, and are silver underneath. The leaves are glossy dark green. It is a useful gap-filler in borders, though it can also be grown in pots. ROBIN REDBREAST is not particularly widely sold, but is by no means hard to find. Minimal pruning is required, but if growth is getting too rampant, cut shoots back to outward-facing buds in late winter. Sideshoots can also be shortened then if necessary.

PLANT PROFILE	
HEIGHT	18in (45cm)
SPREAD	24in (60cm)
TYPE	Groundcover
HARDINESS	Z5–9
FLOWERING	Summer to autumn

R | 'Roger Lambelin'

GIVEN THE WONDERFUL COLORING, with white-edged, crimson-purple petals, and the lovely scent, this Hybrid Perpetual rose is definitely worth a try, but note that deep, rich soil is vital for good growth and a good display. Prepare it well before planting, and add well-rotted compost annually. It sometimes loses its white edges and reverts to red; if this happens, there is nothing you can do to correct it. In formal gardens, prune shoots by one-half to two-thirds in late winter. In less formal and cottage gardens, remove only diseased, dead, and damaged growth, and give a light overall trim for shape.

PLANT PROFILE

HEIGHT	3ft (1m)
SPREAD	3ft (1m)
TYPE	Old garden rose
HARDINESS	Z5–9
FLOWERING	Summer to autumn

ROSE GAUJARD ('Gaumo')

A GOOD FUN ROSE, as popular now as when it was introduced in 1957, ROSE GAUJARD is a lively bush for perking up borders. With 80 petals, the flowers combine cherry red above with pale pink and white beneath, while the leaves are large and glossy. Forget the virtual lack of scent; this rose keeps going without any let-up, and does not lose its color. In late winter, remove all unproductive stems, and prune the rest hard to outward-facing buds at 8–10in (20–25cm). Choosing a bud facing outward helps remove and deter crossing central shoots. For large, showy flowers, prune to two or three buds.

PLANT PROFILE	
HEIGHT 3ft (1m)	
SPREAD 30in (75cm)	
TYPE Bush (large-flowered)	
HARDINESS Z5–9	
FLOWERING Summer to autumn	

R | ROSEMARY HARKNESS ('Harrowbord')

A FAILSAFE ORANGE with a touch of pink, ROSEMARY HARKNESS has a strong scent and good disease resistance, with a reliable show of flowers all summer against bushy, branching, leafy growth. Being on the small side, under 3ft (1m), it should be easy to slot into a gap in the border. It is a good contender for mixed rose plans with either brash colors or quieter pastels. Remove all unproductive stems in late winter, and prune the others hard to outward-facing buds at 8–10in (20–25cm). This helps maintain an open center to the bush. For large, showy flowers, prune to just two or three buds.

PLANT PROFILE

HEIGHT 32in (80cm)

SPREAD 32in (80cm)

TYPE Bush (large-flowered)

HARDINESS Z5–9 H9–5

FLOWERING Summer to autumn

'Roseraie de l'Haÿ'

R

A SUPERB SHRUB that has been a big hit for over 100 years, 'Roseraie de l'Haÿ' has enormous presence. Growth is so bushy and vigorous that it makes a very good hedge or feature at the back of a border. The buds are unusually long and attractive, being colored wine red. When open, the flowers are just over 4in (10cm) wide and rich purple-crimson with a strong scent. Even the leaves are a healthy, fresh green. Usually listed with the Rugosa roses in catalogs, it is excellent in every way. In late winter, prune by one-half to two-thirds; pruning harder gives fewer stems with larger flowers.

PLANT PROFILE	
HEIGHT 7ft (2.2m)	
SPREAD 6ft (2m)	
TYPE Shrub	
HARDINESS Z4–9 H9–1	
FLOWERING Summer to autumn	

R | ROSY CUSHION ('Interall')

THIS MODERN SHRUB IS A GOOD CHOICE for two reasons.
First, it has pale pink, white-eyed, lightly scented flowers (and
the display really is continuous), and second, its dense mass of
prickly, leafy stems makes ground-covering, weed-suppressing
growth. It forms a large, bushy plant nicely softened by the
smallish, open flowers with seven or eight petals each. To
create an impressive shrub, remove only diseased, dead, and
damaged growth. A light late-winter pruning also helps produce
a balanced shape and results in more stems with smaller
blooms. Harder pruning gives fewer stems with larger flowers.

PLANT PROFILE

HEIGHT 3ft (1m)

SPREAD 4ft (1.2m)

TYPE Shrub

HARDINESS Z5–9 H9–5

FLOWERING Summer to autumn

'Rosy Mantle'

R

THE SHAPELY, 4IN- (10CM-) WIDE FLOWERS of 'Rosy Mantle'
are rose to salmon pink, appear in clusters, and have a very
good scent. On the down side, its climbing stems are quite stiff
and do not have that many leaves. For the first two years, train
the new shoots into a horizontal position to produce plenty
of flowering sideshoots. From then on, prune in the autumn
after flowering, nipping back the main stems if necessary and
shortening the sideshoots by about two-thirds.

PLANT PROFILE	
HEIGHT 8ft (2.5m)	
TYPE Climber	
HARDINESS Z5–9 H9–5	
FLOWERING Summer to autumn	

R | *roxburghii* Burr rose, Chestnut rose, Chinquapin rose

THE ONE THING EVERYONE AGREES ON is that this is quirky, stiff-stemmed, colorful, and huge. It makes a robust, impenetrable shape thanks to the rigid growth and vicious prickles beneath the leaves, while the flowers are beautifully rounded and pinkish. They are followed by 1in- (2.5cm-) wide hips, said to look like small, green chestnuts, which gradually turn pale brown. Unlike most roses, it also looks good in winter because of its flaking, yellow-tinged bark. It is ideal for wild or cottage gardens. Remove only diseased, dead, and damaged growth and prune lightly for a balanced shape.

PLANT PROFILE
HEIGHT 6ft (2m)
SPREAD 6ft (2m)
TYPE Wild
HARDINESS Z6–9
FLOWERING Summer; hips in autumn

ROYAL WILLIAM ('Korzaun')

R

THERE ARE SOME EXCELLENT CRIMSON REDS among the large-flowered bush roses, and ROYAL WILLIAM is one of the best. It was voted UK Rose of the Year in 1987, and it is obvious why. The nicely shaped flowers do not get lost in any nearby summer mayhem thanks to their rich red color and size, being 5in (12cm) wide. New buds keep appearing over summer, guaranteeing a good supply, and they are great for cutting. In late winter, remove all unproductive stems, and prune the rest to outward-facing buds at 8–10in (20–25cm). For large, showy flowers, prune to just two or three buds.

PLANT PROFILE

HEIGHT 3ft (1m)

SPREAD 30in (75cm)

TYPE Bush (large-flowered)

HARDINESS Z5–9 H9–5

FLOWERING Summer to autumn

R

'Ruby Wedding'

SOME EXPERTS CALL THIS "respectable," which means that they do not rate it as a must-buy, highly elegant rose, but that it is a perfectly decent red that will not let you down. Growth is bushy and spreading, and thanks to its smallish flowers (which some might call too small), 'Ruby Wedding' adds nicely to the flow in a border where the appearance of the whole rates more highly than individual ingredients. In late winter, remove all unproductive stems, and prune the rest hard to outward-facing buds at 8–10in (20–25cm) or, for large, showy flowers, prune harder to just two or three buds.

PLANT PROFILE

HEIGHT 3ft (1m)

SPREAD 30in (75cm)

TYPE Bush (large-flowered)

HARDINESS Z6–9

FLOWERING Summer

rugosa Hedgehog rose, Japanese rose, Ramanas rose   **R**

MORE ACCURATELY CALLED A WILD SHRUB ROSE, this rose has a range of good features. First, you can grow it in sandy soil and it certainly does not have to be pampered. Second, the dense, vigorous growth makes a thorny, impenetrable hedge with leathery, dark green leaves. Third, the scented flowers give a constant show over summer. Finally, they are followed by tomato-shaped, bright red hips, often with an orange tinge. In formal gardens, prune shoots by one-half to two-thirds in late winter. In less formal and cottage gardens, remove diseased, dead, and damaged growth, and give a light pruning for shape.

PLANT PROFILE
HEIGHT 1–2.5m (3–8ft)
SPREAD 1–2.5m (3–8ft)
TYPE Shrub
HARDINESS Z2–9 H9–1
FLOWERING Summer to autumn; hips in autumn

R | *rugosa* 'Alba'

THE PURE WHITE VERSION of *R. rugosa*, this rose has silky flowers (opening from pinkish buds) all through the summer, which are promptly followed by an excellent show of large, shiny, orange-red hips. *R. rugosa* 'Alba' also has a good covering of bright green foliage and eventually makes a superb shrub. Prune it in late winter, after flowering, by one-half to two-thirds, though in cottage and informal gardens, pruning can be much lighter. In general, harder pruning gives fewer stems with larger flowers, and lighter pruning more flowering stems with smaller blooms.

PLANT PROFILE

HEIGHT 6ft (2m)

SPREAD 6ft (2m)

TYPE Shrub

HARDINESS Z2–9 H9–1

FLOWERING Summer to autumn; hips in autumn

'Salet'

OFTEN LISTED AS A MOSS ROSE, 'Salet' has light mossy growth on the stems and buds. The latter appear in clusters and open to clear pink, summer-long flowers. They have a ruffled, clustered arrangement of petals and exude an old-fashioned charm and a good scent. Introduced in France in 1854, it is a good cottage-garden rose. To create a large shrub, remove only diseased, dead, and damaged growth, and leave the old wood intact. Light late-winter pruning also helps produce a balanced shape and more flowering stems with smaller blooms, while harder pruning gives fewer stems with larger flowers.

PLANT PROFILE

HEIGHT 4ft (1.2m)

SPREAD 3ft (1m)

TYPE Old garden rose

HARDINESS Z4–9

FLOWERING Summer

S | 'Sally Holmes'

ATTRACTIVELY AND UNUSUALLY UPRIGHT, the highly distinctive 'Sally Holmes' sends up strong growth with clusters of scented, creamy white flowers. Each one has five petals and lies open and flat, well clear of the glossy leaves. It has won many awards since it was introduced in 1976, and is very popular. It is beautiful in cottage gardens. Remove only diseased, dead, and damaged growth when pruning. Give a minimal late-winter pruning for a balanced shape if necessary. Harder pruning gives fewer stems with larger flowers, and lighter pruning more flowering stems with smaller blooms.

PLANT PROFILE

HEIGHT	6ft (2m)
SPREAD	3ft (1m)
TYPE	Shrub
HARDINESS	Z5–9
FLOWERING	Summer to autumn

'Sander's White Rambler'

S

ITS BIG ASSET IS THE LATE SUMMER SHOW of smallish flowers in large clusters (when many other roses have stopped), with a fresh, fruity scent. It is excellent for making sure summer goes out with a bang. Since it was introduced in 1912, 'Sander's White Rambler' has been a big favorite, used in a wide range of ways. Grow it up pergolas, over arches, and into trees. In late summer, for the first two years, prune sideshoots by 3in (8cm) to a strong new shoot. From the third year, prune at most one-third of the oldest main stems back to ground level.

PLANT PROFILE	
HEIGHT	12ft (4m)
TYPE	Rambler
HARDINESS	Z5–9
FLOWERING	Late summer

S | 'Sarah van Fleet'

As a THICK, THORNY, IMPENETRABLE, LEAFY HEDGE (keeping out people and animals) or a huge, upright shrub for the back of the border, this Rugosa rose is liberally covered with pink flowers, with just a hint of lilac. They start opening in early summer, with their best show in midsummer, carrying on into autumn. The leaves can suffer from rust, and there are no hips. In formal gardens, prune shoots by one-half to two-thirds in late winter. In less formal and cottage gardens, remove only diseased, dead, and damaged growth, and give a light overall pruning for shape.

PLANT PROFILE

HEIGHT	8ft (2.5m)
SPREAD	5ft (1.5m)
TYPE	Shrub
HARDINESS	Z4–9
FLOWERING	Summer to autumn

SAVOY HOTEL ('Harvintage')

S

THE FLOWERS ARE BEAUTIFULLY SHAPED, the color is soft, light pink, the growth is disease-free and bushy, and the leaves dark green. SAVOY HOTEL is an excellent, all-purpose small rose that gives a continuous supply of flowers over summer, and is ideal in mixed borders, with other roses, and as a cut flower. Introduced in 1989, it has won several top awards. In late winter, remove all unproductive stems, and prune the rest hard to outward-facing buds at 8–10in (20–25cm). This helps remove crisscrossing shoots in the center. For large, showy flowers, prune harder, leaving just two or three buds.

PLANT PROFILE	
HEIGHT	32in (80cm)
SPREAD	24in (60cm)
TYPE	Bush (large-flowered)
HARDINESS	Z5–9
FLOWERING	Summer to autumn

S   'Scabrosa'

MAKING AN IMPRESSIVELY DENSE, bushy, free-flowering, healthy hedge or shrub for the back of the border, 'Scabrosa' is a Rugosa rose highly rated for its ability to flower freely right through summer. Each bloom is 4in (10cm) wide or more, being followed by a good show of large, round, orange-red hips. It is sometimes listed as *R. rugosa* 'Scabrosa'. In formal gardens, prune shoots by one-half to two-thirds in late winter. In less formal and cottage gardens, remove only diseased, dead, and damaged growth, and give a light overall trim for shape.

PLANT PROFILE

HEIGHT 5½ft (1.7m)

SPREAD 5½ft (1.7m)

TYPE Shrub

HARDINESS Z2–9

FLOWERING Summer to autumn; hips in autumn

'Scharlachglut'

ITS TRANSLATED NAME, SCARLET FIRE, (which is how it is often listed) gives a much clearer idea of what to expect from this rose: a midsummer blast of blazing, flashy scarlet flowers, each one 5in (12cm) wide with golden yellow in the middle, adding plenty of zip. The flowers are followed by large red hips. Though 'Scharlachglut' is used as a massive shrub, it can be trained to grow up against a wall. To create a large, impressive shrub, remove only diseased, dead, and damaged growth, and give a light pruning in winter for shape. Harder pruning gives fewer stems with larger flowers.

PLANT PROFILE

HEIGHT To 10ft (3m)

SPREAD 6ft (2m)

TYPE Shrub

HARDINESS Z4–9

FLOWERING Summer; hips in autumn

S

'Schoolgirl'

A SLIGHTLY QUIRKY NAME for this lanky, stiff-stemmed, branching climber. Its 4in- (10cm-) wide, shapely flowers are richly scented and look just as good after days of heavy rain. The deep apricot (nearly orange) color is a boon since few other climbers have it, and the only minor fault is the sparseness of its leaves. It can be trained up any structure, from walls to pergolas. For the first two years, train new shoots into a horizontal position. From the third year, prune in the autumn, after flowering, nipping back the main stems if necessary and shortening sideshoots by two-thirds.

PLANT PROFILE

HEIGHT 10ft (3m)

TYPE Climber

HARDINESS Z5–9

FLOWERING Summer to autumn

'Seagull'

S

FIRING UP RAMPANT, ARCHING STEMS, 'Seagull' scrambles high into sturdy old trees, where it produces large clusters of gold-centered small flowers, 1in (2.5cm) wide. It is irrelevant that the leaves are grayish green because they mix in with those of the support tree. It can also be grown up pergolas and arches. In late summer, for the first two years, prune sideshoots by 3in (8cm) to a strong new shoot. From the third year, prune at most one-third of the oldest main stems back to ground level.

PLANT PROFILE
HEIGHT 6m (20ft)
TYPE Rambler
HARDINESS Z5–9
FLOWERING Summer

S

sericea subsp. *omeiensis* f. *pteracantha* Winged thorn rose

FIRST, IGNORE THE IMPOSSIBLE NAME (most people just call it
R. pteracantha) and second, look at one before you buy. This
rose has the most fantastic, flattish triangular thorns lined up
along the stems, but they are vicious and not for gardens with
children. The thorns can be ⅞in (2cm) high and over 1in
(2.5cm) wide at the base. Because they are reddish and
translucent, make sure that the sun can shine through them.
The few summer flowers are virtually irrelevant. A hard late-
winter prune (to promote new growth) is vital because the
thorns lose their color in their second summer.

PLANT PROFILE	
HEIGHT	8ft (2.5m)
SPREAD	7ft (2.2m)
TYPE	Wild
HARDINESS	Z6–9 H9–5
FLOWERING	Summer

SEXY REXY ('Macrexy')

S

IT MIGHT SELL MORE ON ITS NAME than its flowers, but that does not stop them from being very attractive. They are a gentle, soft pink and packed with petals on strong, healthy growth. The buds appear in large clusters. Make sure you promptly snip off the fading flowers to promote even more to follow. SEXY REXY makes a good gift because it is thoroughly reliable in every way. In late winter, cut back the main stems to 10–18in (25–45cm) above the ground, and reduce sideshoots by about one-third of their length.

PLANT PROFILE	
HEIGHT 28in (70cm)	
SPREAD 24in (60cm)	
TYPE Bush (cluster-flowered)	
HARDINESS Z6–9 H9–6	
FLOWERING Summer to autumn	

S | SHARIFA ASMA ('Ausreef')

SHORT AND EXQUISITE, this 1989 introduction injects old-world charm into a repeat-flowering rose with soft pink flowers, paler pink at the edge. They are almost translucent, with a dash of yellow at the base. If that makes it sound like a delicate plant, it is not—growth is quite vigorous, bushy, and compact. It makes a classy addition to formal and cottage gardens. In late winter, prune shoots by one-half to two-thirds, pruning harder for fewer stems with larger flowers, and more lightly for more flowering stems with smaller blooms.

PLANT PROFILE

HEIGHT 3ft (1m)

SPREAD 30in (75cm)

TYPE Shrub

HARDINESS Z6–9

FLOWERING Summer

SHEILA'S PERFUME ('Harsherry')

S

THE SECOND PART OF THE NAME is perfectly accurate. There is a strong perfume (confirmed by two awards for fragrance), though the color may not be quite to everyone's liking. The large, shapely flowers are yellow with red running unevenly around the edges. The blooms appear individually or in clusters set against the abundant, disease-resistant, glossy, dark green leaves. Cut back the main stems in late winter to 10–18in (25–45cm), and reduce the sideshoots by about one-third of their length.

PLANT PROFILE	
HEIGHT	30in (75cm)
SPREAD	24in (60cm)
TYPE	Bush (cluster-flowered)
HARDINESS	Z5–9
FLOWERING	Summer to autumn

S | 'Silver Jubilee'

NOT ONLY A BEAUTIFUL MIX of three colors—pink, apricot-peach, and cream (which do not fade)—this rose also has petals perfectly arranged in symmetrical circles. There is a lovely scent, and the 5in- (12cm-) wide flowers keep appearing over summer. Growth is dense and leafy. Introduced in 1978, 'Silver Jubilee' later picked up four top rose awards. In late winter, remove all unproductive stems, and prune the rest hard to outward-facing buds at 8–10in (20–25cm). This helps remove crisscrossing shoots in the center. For large, showy flowers, prune harder, to just two or three buds.

PLANT PROFILE

HEIGHT 3½ft (1.1m)

SPREAD 24in (60cm)

TYPE Bush (large-flowered)

HARDINESS Z5–9 H9–5

FLOWERING Summer to autumn

'Silver Wedding'

IT WILL CERTAINLY MAKE A GOOD GIFT, and this rose is far from being a novelty buy. The flowers have a nice symmetrical shape, though with barely any scent, and appear in clusters over the summer. The distinguishing feature of 'Silver Wedding' is its small size, not far from that of a miniature rose. It can be grown in pots or tucked into a small gap in a border. In late winter, remove all the unproductive stems, and prune the remainder to outward-facing buds, leaving 8–10in (20–25cm) of stem above the ground. For large, showy flowers, prune harder, to two or three buds.

PLANT PROFILE	
HEIGHT 20in (50cm)	
SPREAD 20in (50cm)	
TYPE Bush (large-flowered)	
HARDINESS Z5–9	
FLOWERING Summer to autumn	

S | SIMBA ('Korbelma')

AN EXCELLENT ROSE FOR CUT FLOWERS, each large bloom is very stylish, with a high point. The flowers usually appear singly instead of in groups, withstand poor weather, and repeat through summer with a few gaps between each burst of buds. The British named this rose after a dog, SIMBA, but American growers may call it GOLDSMITH. Remove all unproductive stems in late winter, and prune the remainder hard to outward-facing buds at 8–10in (20–25cm). For larger flowers, prune harder, leaving just two or three buds.

PLANT PROFILE

HEIGHT 24in (60cm)

SPREAD 20in (50cm)

TYPE Bush (large-flowered)

HARDINESS Z5–9 H9–5

FLOWERING Summer to autumn

'Sombreuil'

THIS OLD-FASHIONED ROSE has blooms with a flat, crinkled, ruffled look, creamy white with a dash of pale pink in the middle. There is a gorgeous sweet scent all summer from the continuous supply of flowers, while the leaves are lush green. Grow it against a sunny wall for the best effect. With pruning, 'Sombreuil' can become a shorter, dense, bushy shrub. To grow it as a climber, train new shoots into a horizontal position for the first two years. From then on, prune in autumn, after flowering, nipping back the main stems if they are too long and shortening sideshoots by two-thirds.

S

PLANT PROFILE

HEIGHT	12ft (4m)
TYPE	Climber
HARDINESS	Z6–9
FLOWERING	Summer

S | 'Southampton'

ITS RED–FLUSHED, APRICOT–ORANGE COLOR, leafy bushiness, and the totally satisfying shape of the high-pointed flowers have made 'Southampton' very popular with the public and impressed the rose experts. The flowers are clearly on display all summer, appearing either individually or in clusters on firm stems, and provide good impact in a border. The glossy green foliage is disease-resistant. In late winter, cut back the main stems to about 10–18in (25–45cm) above the ground, and reduce the sideshoots by about one-third of their length.

PLANT PROFILE

HEIGHT 3½ft (1.1m)

SPREAD 28in (70cm)

TYPE Bush (cluster-flowered)

HARDINESS Z5–9 H9–5

FLOWERING Summer to autumn

'Souvenir de la Malmaison'

NAMED AFTER THE EMPRESS JOSEPHINE'S great French rose garden, this Bourbon rose lives up to its name. The large, 15in-(2cm-) wide flowers have the typical old-garden-rose, petal-packed, crumpled-ruffled look and deliver a lovely scent. Its repeat summer-flowering means it is quite capable of standing alone, in its own bed, on a lawn. It looks miserable after heavy rain, when the sodden flowers hang down, but that is only a brief hiccup. Some catalogs give its height and width as 3 ft (1m), but it will spread to 5ft (1.5m). In late winter, prune shoots by one-half to two-thirds.

PLANT PROFILE	
HEIGHT To 5ft (1.5m)	
SPREAD To 5ft (1.5m)	
TYPE Old garden rose	
HARDINESS Z6–9 H9–6	
FLOWERING Summer to autumn	

S

'Souvenir de Saint Anne's'

CLOSELY RELATED TO 'SOUVENIR DE LA MALMAISON' (*see page 273*), many consider this rose slightly superior. The flowers are more shapely and do not get that hangdog look after heavy rain, and they have a stronger scent, which apparently emanates from the stamens. It is also slightly more vigorous, taller, and bushier. A Bourbon rose, it was found growing in Ireland, near Dublin. In late winter, prune the stems by one-half to two-thirds. Harder pruning gives fewer stems with larger flowers, while lighter pruning results in more flowering stems with slightly smaller blooms.

PLANT PROFILE

HEIGHT 5ft (1.5m)

SPREAD 5ft (1.5m)

TYPE Old garden rose

HARDINESS Z6–9

FLOWERING Summer to autumn

'Souvenir du Docteur Jamain'

S

THE VELVETY PETALS are a deep, dark, wine red color with just a hint of purple. To maintain this rich color, keep it out of direct sun or the impact is lost, and the petals turn brownish red. The scent is strong and the first batch of flowers is the best. Dating back to to 1865, it is a sumptuous rose, with dark green leaves, and is worth pampering. It can also be grown as a 10ft- (3m-) high wall climber. In formal gardens, prune shoots by one-half to two-thirds in late winter. In less formal and cottage gardens, remove only diseased, dead, and damaged growth, and give a light overall pruning for shape.

PLANT PROFILE

HEIGHT	6ft (2m)
SPREAD	4ft (1.2m)
TYPE	Old garden rose
HARDINESS	Z5–9
FLOWERING	Midsummer and autumn

S

'Stanwell Perpetual'

FOUND BY ACCIDENT and introduced in 1838, this rose has been a big favorite in cottage gardens ever since. The pale pink flowers have an open shape and are loosely formed, appearing off-and-on over summer, and the scent is on the strong side. Its twiggy, arching growth is very prickly, and the gray-green leaves are small and ferny. It is highly effective in a free, informal planting plan. Remove diseased, dead, and damaged growth, but leave the old wood intact. A minimal late-winter pruning also helps produce a balanced shape.

PLANT PROFILE

HEIGHT	3ft (1m)
SPREAD	4ft (1.2m)
TYPE	Wild
HARDINESS	Z3–9
FLOWERING	Summer to autumn

SUMMER WINE ('Korinzont')

THE CORAL-PINK, SCENTED FLOWERS, with a dash of red in the center, appear on stiff, branching, upright growth, which should easily cover a medium-size wall, even in shade. SUMMER WINE can also be trained up and around pillars, posts, and arches. Training the stems into the horizontal (if possible) forces up even more flowering growth. The display lasts all summer. From the third year, prune in the autumn after flowering, nipping back overlong main stems and shortening sideshoots by two-thirds.

PLANT PROFILE	
HEIGHT 10ft (3m)	
TYPE Climber	
HARDINESS Z5–9	
FLOWERING Summer to autumn	

SUNBLEST ('Landora')

A FIRST-RATE, ALL-PURPOSE, BRIGHT YELLOW ROSE, it has a compact shape, reliably flowers all summer, and provides plenty of cut stems. Each bloom is on the large side, at 3½in (9cm) wide, has pointed petals, and is set against a background of glossy leaves. There might be occasional attacks of blackspot, but that certainly should not deter amateur growers. In late winter, remove all unproductive stems, and prune the rest hard to outward-facing buds at 8–10in (20–25cm). This helps keep the center clear of crossing shoots. For large, showy flowers, prune harder, leaving just two or three buds.

PLANT PROFILE

HEIGHT	3ft (1m)
SPREAD	24in (60cm)
TYPE	Bush (large-flowered)
HARDINESS	Z5–9
FLOWERING	Summer to autumn

SUNSET BOULEVARD ('Harbabble')

VOTED UK ROSE OF THE YEAR IN 1997, SUNSET BOULEVARD is a high-quality, compact plant with attractive buds producing warm pink flowers. There is almost no let-up in the show over summer and, despite the lack of scent, its other qualities make it an excellent choice for gaps at the front of a border. Do not crowd it too much with adjacent plants or the stylish, shapely flowers might get obscured. In late winter, cut back the main stems to approximately 10–18in (25–45cm) above ground, and shorten the sideshoots by about one-third.

S

PLANT PROFILE	
HEIGHT	3ft (1m)
SPREAD	24in (60cm)
TYPE	Bush (cluster-flowered)
HARDINESS	Z6–9
FLOWERING	Summer to autumn

S | SURREY ('Korlanum')

ONE OF THE MOST EFFECTIVE groundcover roses, SURREY covers a decent area with a mound of dense, leafy growth and stems. Hardly any weeds will grow through it. The flowering is equally good, with warm pink blooms all summer and a nice scent. It makes a very effective low shape in front of taller plants. In very large gardens, you can even use it in spreading drifts. Minimal pruning is needed, but if growth is getting too rampant, cut back the main shoots to outward-facing buds in late winter and reduce sideshoots at the same time.

PLANT PROFILE

HEIGHT 32in (80cm)

SPREAD 4ft (1.2m)

TYPE Groundcover

HARDINESS Z5–9

FLOWERING Summer to autumn

SWANY ('Meiburenac')

S

MAKE SURE YOU HAVE ROOM for SWANY's vigorous, dense, groundcover growth, packed with glossy, dark green leaves. It is too big a spreader for borders but will effectively block out weeds on a spare patch of sunny ground. There are profuse clusters of small white flowers all summer, though you will have to get very close to notice any scent. Little pruning is needed. If growth is too rampant, cut back the main and sideshoots to outward-facing buds in late winter.

PLANT PROFILE

HEIGHT 30in (75cm)

SPREAD To 5½ft (1.7m)

TYPE Groundcover

HARDINESS Z5–9

FLOWERING Summer to autumn

SWEET DREAM ('Fryminicot')

THE ROSE BREEDERS' ROSE OF THE YEAR in 1988, it is still a top buy, with a range of virtues. SWEET DREAM has a gorgeous peach-apricot color that does not fade, the flowers are good at withstanding the rain, and there is neat, leafy, bushy growth. You can grow this versatile patio rose wherever you want—in pots, at the foot of tall structures or ornamental objects, or to encircle larger feature plants. In late winter, cut out all growth apart from the strongest shoots, and then cut them back by about one-third to one-half. This regimen forces up plenty of new, vigorous growth.

PLANT PROFILE

HEIGHT 16in (40cm)

SPREAD 14in (35cm)

TYPE Bush (cluster-flowered, patio)

HARDINESS Z3–9 H9–1

FLOWERING Summer to autumn

SWEET JULIET ('Ausleap')

COMBINING OLD GARDEN ROSE–TYPE FLOWERS with plenty of vigor, SWEET JULIET has fresh buds all summer long, producing a lovely show of apricot-yellow flowers. New growth has a tendency to appear just about anywhere, including right at the base, creating a dense tangle of stems. All this energetic growth invariably means more stems than flowers, but heavy pruning restores the balance. The leaves are long and pointed. In late winter, prune stems by one-half to two-thirds. Harder pruning gives fewer stems with larger flowers, and lighter pruning more stems with smaller blooms.

S

PLANT PROFILE

HEIGHT 4ft (1.2m)

SPREAD 3ft (1m)

TYPE Shrub

HARDINESS Z5–9

FLOWERING Summer to autumn

S | SWEET MAGIC ('Dicmagic')

ENGLAND'S ROYAL NATIONAL ROSE SOCIETY voted this Rose of the Year in 1987. It has an excellent supply of apricot orange flowers (with a dash of yellow, which increases as the flowers fade), set against bright green leaves. Hips follow the flowers. It looks equally good whether grown in pots, as edging, or right at the front of a border. You do not need a green thumb to grow SWEET MAGIC. In late winter, remove all growth except for the strongest shoots, and cut these back by one-third to one-half. This regimen forces up plenty of new, vigorous, twiggy growth.

PLANT PROFILE

HEIGHT 18in (45cm)

SPREAD 18in (45cm)

TYPE Bush (cluster-flowered, patio)

HARDINESS Z5–9 H9–5

FLOWERING Summer to autumn; hips in autumn

'Sympathie'

THE FIRST FLUSH OF FLOWERS is the best, producing deep, dark red blooms in heavy clusters. They are borne on free-branching, arching stems covered with dark green leaves. More flowers follow and compensate for the lack of scent. It is equally successful against walls and growing over arches. For the first two years, train new shoots into a horizontal position to produce flowering sideshoots. From the third year, prune in the autumn, after flowering, nipping back the main stems if necessary and shortening sideshoots by two-thirds.

PLANT PROFILE	
HEIGHT	10ft (3m)
TYPE	Climber
HARDINESS	Z5–9 H9–5
FLOWERING	Summer to autumn

T | TANGO ('Macfirwal')

ALSO KNOWN AS STRETCH JOHNSON, TANGO is a highly distinctive rose. The flowers are bright orange-red, with yellow in the center and yellowish white around the rim of the petals. The ebullient effect (a bit much for some) is enhanced because the flowers appear in large clusters. Make sure it suits your color scheme. Introduced in 1988, it promptly won a Royal National Rose Society Gold Medal in England. Cut back the main stems in late winter to 10–18in (25–45cm), and shorten sideshoots by about one-third.

PLANT PROFILE

HEIGHT 30in (75cm)

SPREAD 24in (60cm)

TYPE Bush (cluster-flowered)

HARDINESS Z5–9

FLOWERING Summer to autumn

TEQUILA SUNRISE ('Dicobey')

A FLASHY, POPULAR, BRIGHTLY COLORED ROSE, it has sprays of
4in- (10cm-) wide, yellow flowers with scarlet running along
the tips of the petals. They keep going through the summer.
Growth is quite bushy and vigorous, and the leaves are glossy,
dark green. If you need an eye-catching rose at the front of
the border, put it high on your list. In late winter, remove all
the unproductive stems, and prune the rest hard to outward-
facing buds at 8–10in (20–25cm). This helps remove
crisscrossing shoots in the center. For large, showy flowers,
prune harder, to just two or three buds.

PLANT PROFILE

HEIGHT 30in (75cm)

SPREAD 24in (60cm)

TYPE Bush (large-flowered)

HARDINESS Z5–9

FLOWERING Summer to autumn

T

'The Fairy'

'THE FAIRY' HAS EVERYTHING GOING FOR IT, except that flowering does not begin until the second half of summer. If you can wait, you get wonderfully bushy, mounded growth covered by clusters of tiny buds that open to small, light pink flowers, giving an informal, cottage-garden show. It can be grown as a shrub, a hedge, or even in a large tub. It is also highly effective as a standard. When pruning, remove only diseased, dead, and damaged growth. A minimal late-winter pruning also helps produce a balanced shape. If you want fewer stems with larger flowers, prune harder.

PLANT PROFILE

HEIGHT	24–36in (60–90cm)
SPREAD	24–36in (60–90cm)
TYPE	Shrub
HARDINESS	Z5–9 H9–5
FLOWERING	Late summer to autumn

'The Garland'

T

AN OLD, IMPRESSIVE RAMBLER, dating back to 1835, it has a strong, fruity scent. The once-a-summer profusion of pinkish white buds opens to small, white, flat flowers with a yellow eye. They look a bit like daisies and make a terrific display, standing out against the almost dark green leaves. 'The Garland' can be grown up the trunks of sturdy old trees, or allowed to pile up, making a big, baggy, informal shrub. In late summer, for the first two years, prune sideshoots by 3in (8cm) to a strong new shoot. From the thrid year, prune at most one-third of the oldest main stems back to ground level.

PLANT PROFILE	
HEIGHT 15ft (5m)	
TYPE Rambler	
HARDINESS Z6–9	
FLOWERING Midsummer	

T | THE PILGRIM ('Auswalker')

IF YOU LIKE THE YELLOW ROSE GRAHAM THOMAS (*see page 135*), you may also want THE PILGRIM, which was raised from it. There is a lovely mix of scented, soft yellow flowers, pale in the center and almost white around the outside. The look is of an old garden rose, but the vigor matches a modern one. Growth is nicely upright, and it can also be trained as a modest climber, reaching 8ft (2.5m). In late winter, prune stems by one-half to two-thirds. Harder pruning gives fewer stems with larger flowers, and lighter pruning more stems with smaller blooms.

PLANT PROFILE

HEIGHT 3½ft (1.1m)

SPREAD 3ft (1m)

TYPE Shrub

HARDINESS Z6–9

FLOWERING Summer

'The Queen Elizabeth'

ALSO KNOWN SIMPLY AS QUEEN ELIZABETH, this is one bush rose that definitely needs to go right at the back of the border because it shoots up over head-height. The leaves are impressively large, leathery, dark green, and glossy, and the whole plant is so sturdy and upright that it can also be grown as a decent hedge. It was voted the World's Favorite Rose in 1979 and remains a top-class plant. In late winter, cut back the main stems to 10–18in (25–45cm) above ground, and shorten the sideshoots by about two-thirds.

T

PLANT PROFILE

HEIGHT To 7ft (2.2m)

SPREAD 3ft (1m)

TYPE Bush (cluster-flowered)

HARDINESS Z5–9 H9–5

FLOWERING Summer to autumn

T | THE TIMES ROSE ('Korpeahn')

FOR A REGULAR SUPPLY OF CRIMSON FLOWERS all summer on a modest-sized, disease-resistant bush rose, this one is hard to beat. The color is bright, and the dark green leaves (reddish bronze when young) provide an effective background. Plant it at the foot of a pergola with climbers shooting up past it, at the front of a border, or wherever you need an attention-grabbing rose. In late winter, cut back the main stems to 10–18in (25–45cm), and reduce the sideshoots by about one-third of their length.

PLANT PROFILE

HEIGHT 24in (60cm)

SPREAD 30in (75cm)

TYPE Bush (cluster-flowered)

HARDINESS Z5–9 H9–5

FLOWERING Summer to autumn

TOP MARKS ('Fryministar')

CHOCK FULL OF SMALL VERMILION FLOWERS, this compact plant has a huge presence. The flowers hang on well, keeping their intense color, but if you really want them to stand out, plant TOP MARKS in a pot, giving it a prominent position. It is also excellent in patio gardens and for edging paths. The leaves are glossy and healthy. In late winter, remove all growth except the strongest shoots, and then cut them back by one-third to one-half. This forces up plenty of new, vigorous growth.

T

PLANT PROFILE	
HEIGHT 18in (45cm)	
SPREAD 18in (45cm)	
TYPE Bush (cluster-flowered, patio)	
HARDINESS Z6–9	
FLOWERING Summer	

T | 'Tour de Malakoff'

IF YOU ARE CREATING AN OLD ROSE GARDEN specializing in large flowers and good scent, try this. The flowers are 5in (12cm) wide and well scented, initially with a mix of purple and red (and a dash of gold in the middle), then turning violet and gray. A fine old Centifolia rose, dating back to 1856, it has arching growth that often needs support. When pruning, remove only diseased, dead, and damaged growth, and leave the old wood. A minimal late-winter pruning yields a balanced shape and more stems with smaller blooms, while harder pruning gives fewer stems with larger flowers.

PLANT PROFILE

HEIGHT 6ft (2m)

SPREAD 5ft (1.5m)

TYPE Old garden rose

HARDINESS Z4–9 H9–1

FLOWERING Midsummer

TROIKA ('Poumidor')

SOMETIMES KNOWN AS ROYAL DANE, this has large, 6in-(15cm-) wide, nicely scented flowers with a high center. The color is showy and eye-catching, a good choice for bright and brash schemes, or for the focal point in a quieter plan. Growth is vigorous and tall, with glossy, dark green leaves, making a perfectly reliable rose. In late winter, remove all the unproductive stems, and prune the rest hard to outward-facing buds, leaving 8–10in (20–25cm) of stem. This helps eliminate crossing shoots in the center of the bush. For large, showy flowers, prune harder, leaving just two or three buds.

PLANT PROFILE

HEIGHT 3ft (1m)

SPREAD 30in (75cm)

TYPE Bush (large-flowered)

HARDINESS Z5–9 H9–5

FLOWERING Summer to autumn

T | ## TRUMPETER ('Mactru')

A LIVELY BLAST OF TOMATO ORANGE-RED FLOWERS lasts all summer, into autumn. Growth is neat and compact, with a nice backing of rich, green foliage, and disease is not a problem. TRUMPETER scores high marks at the front of a border where it can be clearly seen. It can also be grown in a circle around an ornamental object (such as a classical, formal staute), or in rows to flank the edge of a path. In late winter, cut back the main stems to 10–18in (25–45cm), and reduce the sideshoots by about one-third of their length.

PLANT PROFILE

HEIGHT 24in (60cm)

SPREAD 20in (50cm)

TYPE Bush (cluster-flowered)

HARDINESS Z5–9 H9–5

FLOWERING Summer to autumn

'Tuscany Superb' Double velvet rose

THE DEEP, RICH RED VELVETY PETALS, gradually fading to purple, make this a wonderful rose, especially since there is a dash of gold in the eye of the flowers. Growth is relatively thornless, strong, and bushy. It is often listed under Gallica roses in catalogs. When pruning, remove only diseased, dead, and damaged growth, and leave the old wood. Give it a minimal late-winter pruning for a balanced shape. The harder you prune, the fewer the stems and the larger the flowers, while lighter pruning gives more stems with smaller blooms.

PLANT PROFILE

HEIGHT 3ft (1m)

SPREAD 3ft (1m)

TYPE Old garden rose

HARDINESS Z3–9 H9–1

FLOWERING Midsummer

V | VALENCIA ('Koreklia')

BETTER IN A COTTAGE OR INFORMAL GARDEN because of its slightly uneven, sprawling growth, VALENCIA scores high marks for its large, 4in- (10cm-) wide, scented flowers. The high-centered, long-stemmed flowers (excellent for cutting) have a hint of copper, and are nicely set off by the leathery, glossy, dark green leaves. The display lasts into autumn. In late winter, prune out all the unproductive stems, and cut the rest back to outward-facing buds at 8–10in (20–25cm). This helps deter crossing shoots in the center. For large, showy flowers, prune to just two or three buds.

PLANT PROFILE

HEIGHT 30in (75cm)

SPREAD 26in (65cm)

TYPE Bush (large-flowered)

HARDINESS Z5–9

FLOWERING Summer to autumn

VALENTINE HEART ('Dicogle')

V

THE BUDS SUGGEST SCARLET FLOWERS but they actually turn out to be pink with a hint of lilac, and have distinctive, frilly petals. The leaves are purple when young, and then turn dark green. The effect is of a small, beautiful, free-and-easy display just right for the front of a bed where its growth can edge on to a path. The long summer show means it is worth buying several plants and lining them up in a row. In late winter, cut back the main stems to 10–18in (25–45cm), and reduce sideshoots by one-third of their length.

PLANT PROFILE

HEIGHT 24in (60cm)

SPREAD 20in (50cm)

TYPE Bush (cluster-flowered)

HARDINESS Z5–9

FLOWERING Summer to autumn

V 'Variegata di Bologna'

OFTEN CALLED A STRIPED ROSE, this has a creamy white flower with reddish markings and stripes in an irregular pattern, like a great big scoop of raspberry ripple ice cream. There is just one show of flowers, worth waiting for and never too garish. Growth is quite strong and vigorous, which means it can be trained as a short climber. 'Variegata di Bologna' is often listed as a Bourbon rose in catalogs. To create a large shrub, remove only diseased, dead, and damaged growth, and leave the old wood intact. A minimal late-winter pruning helps to create a balanced shape.

PLANT PROFILE

HEIGHT 7ft (2.2m)

SPREAD 5ft (1.5m)

TYPE Old garden rose

HARDINESS Z6–9 H9–6

FLOWERING Summer to autumn

'Veilchenblau'

A BIG HIT WITH ROSE EXPERTS, this has thornless stems and sprays of small, scented flowers that change color. The buds are reddish purple, and the opening flowers are maroon-purple with white. They turn bluish lilac and fade to lilac-gray on about the third day. 'Veilchenblau' needs the right background to stand out, and will be lost against the likes of a gray stone wall. Try growing it up a pergola with a rich red and a white climber. For the first two years, prune sideshoots by 3in (8cm) to a strong shoot in late summer. From the third year, prune up to one-third of the oldest stems to the ground.

PLANT PROFILE	
HEIGHT 12ft (4m)	
TYPE Rambler	
HARDINESS Z5–9 H9–5	
FLOWERING Midsummer	

V | *virginiana*

FROM NORTH AMERICA, the wild *R. virginiana* tolerates most soils, including the light and sandy. It produces bushy, shrubby growth and is thick with glossy leaves, producing clear pink, scented flowers. It is at its best in autumn, when the leaves turn beet red as the cold comes, changing to yellow-orange. There is also a good show of round, orange hips. Give it a prominent position. Remove only diseased, dead, and damaged growth, and leave the old wood intact. A minimal late-winter pruning helps to promote a balanced shape.

PLANT PROFILE
HEIGHT 4ft (1.2m)
SPREAD 4ft (1.2m)
TYPE Wild
HARDINESS Z3–9
FLOWERING Midsummer; hips in autumn

WARM WELCOME ('Chewizz')

W

THIS BELONGS TO THE GROUP of modest climbers that are ideal for small walls, or short pillars and posts. The clusters of small flowers cover the plant from top to bottom, giving a good show all through the summer months, while its disease-resistant leaves have a glossy shine. WARM WELCOME can be pruned to restrict height, but will react by putting up more climbing shoots right from the base, making the rose much bushier. It is best to leave well enough alone. Train the new shoots horizontally to produce plenty of flowering sideshoots.

PLANT PROFILE	
HEIGHT 7ft (2.2m)	
TYPE Climber	
HARDINESS Z5–9	
FLOWERING Summer to autumn	

W | WARM WISHES ('Fryxotic')

A FAIL-SAFE CHOICE for a warm peachy color, this rose is well known for its ability to keep flowering over summer and withstand the worst of the weather. In some countries it goes by the name of SUNSET CELEBRATION, a good indication of its color. Growth is strong and bushy, with dark green leaves. Position it in gaps at the front of the border or in a special rose garden. Remove all the unproductive stems in late winter, and prune the rest hard to outward-facing buds at 8–10in (20–25cm). For large, showy flowers, prune harder, leaving just two or three buds.

PLANT PROFILE

HEIGHT	30in (75cm)
SPREAD	24in (60cm)
TYPE	Bush (large-flowered)
HARDINESS	Z6–9
FLOWERING	Summer

'Wedding Day'

W

A GIANT OF A RAMBLER, it needs a huge, sturdy tree to scramble up, or let it loose in a hedgerow. It is a fine sight in midsummer, with its large clusters of opening yellowish buds, followed by wonderfully citrus-scented, creamy white small flowers with yellow in the center. 'Wedding Day' is a better version than its parent, which was found wild in China. Do not be surprised if it exceeds its suggested growth by another 10ft (3m). In late summer, for the first two years, prune sideshoots by 3in (8cm) to a new shoot. From the third year, prune up to one-third of the old main stems to ground level.

PLANT PROFILE	
HEIGHT	25ft (8m)
TYPE	Rambler
HARDINESS	Z5–9 H9–1
FLOWERING	Midsummer

W | WEE JOCK ('Cocabest')

SMALL AND COMPACT, this has two key selling points. The buds are high-pointed, and the petal-packed flowers are deep crimson. They are not that prolific, appearing in reasonable-sized clusters, but the color is so strong that WEE JOCK immediately grabs the eye. It can be used as edging, or placed at the front of a border. It is also a good choice for brightening up sunny courtyard gardens. In late winter, remove all growth except for the strongest shoots, and then cut them back by one-third to one-half. This regimen forces up plenty of new, vigorous growth.

PLANT PROFILE

HEIGHT 14in (35cm)

SPREAD 14in (35cm)

TYPE Bush (cluster-flowered, miniature)

HARDINESS Z5–9 H9–5

FLOWERING Summer to autumn

W

WESTERLAND ('Korwest')

A VIGOROUS, STIFF-STEMMED, UPRIGHT SHRUB, this can also be trained against a wall as a climber, when it can reach 8ft (2.5m) high. Its clusters of scented flowers are brightly colored, with a touch of yellow, and there is barely any let-up over summer. The leaves are dark green. If you grow it as a climber, try to put it against a white wall to bring out the contrast of dark green leaves and orange flowers. To create a large shrub, remove diseased, dead, and damaged growth, and prune lightly for shape in late winter. Harder pruning gives fewer stems with larger flowers.

PLANT PROFILE	
HEIGHT 6ft (2m)	
SPREAD 4ft (1.2m)	
TYPE Shrub	
HARDINESS Z5–9	
FLOWERING Summer to autumn	

W | WHISKY MAC ('Tanky')

ITS BEAUTIFUL MERGING OF YELLOWISH GOLD and amber petals stands out in the border like a flame against its dark green leaves. The scent is mild, the flowers large at 4in (10cm) wide, and the only possible setback is that it is on the tender side; a sunny, sheltered site and good soil are vital. Some say it is unreliable after a few years, but the best advice is to give it a try because it really is quite special. In late winter, remove all unproductive stems, and prune the rest hard to outward-facing buds at 8–10in (20–25cm). This helps remove crisscrossing shoots. For larger flowers, prune to two or three buds.

PLANT PROFILE

HEIGHT	30in (75cm)
SPREAD	24in (60cm)
TYPE	Bush (large-flowered)
HARDINESS	Z5–9
FLOWERING	Summer to autumn

'White Cockade'

A THOROUGHLY RESTRAINED CLIMBER, 'White Cockade' has beautifully shaped white flowers, excellent for cutting. The scent is mild. Growth is on the shrubby side, with dark green leaves, giving good coverage against a smallish wall. 'White Cockade' is also a smart choice for growing up around the legs of a pergola. For the first two years, train new shoots into a horizontal position to produce flowering sideshoots. From then on, prune in the autumn, after flowering, nipping back overlong main stems and shortening sideshoots by two-thirds.

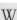

PLANT PROFILE

HEIGHT 7ft (2.2m)

TYPE Climber

HARDINESS Z5–9

FLOWERING Summer to autumn

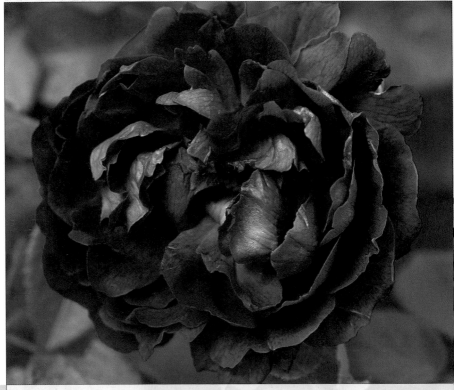

W | 'William Lobb'

THIS MOSS ROSE DOES A QUICK COLOR CHANGE: the flowers open deep, rich purple but, within a day, are lavender-gray, giving the whole shrub a two-tone appearance. Because of its rich scent, it is best grown in a sheltered spot where the smell hangs in the air. It makes a good companion in most plantings with its arching stems, and can even be grown against a sunny wall. Remove only diseased, dead, and damaged growth. A minimal late-winter pruning also helps produce a balanced shape and plenty of flowering stems with smaller blooms. Harder pruning gives fewer stems with larger flowers.

PLANT PROFILE

HEIGHT 6ft (2m)

SPREAD 6ft (2m)

TYPE Old garden rose

HARDINESS Z4–9 H9–1

FLOWERING Early summer

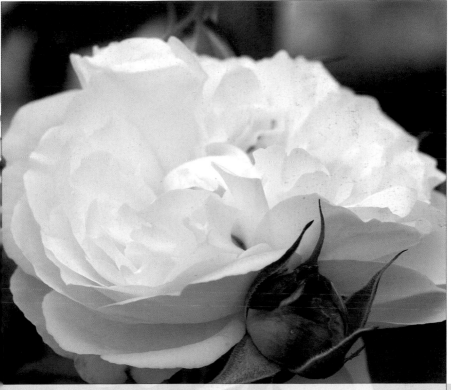

WINCHESTER CATHEDRAL ('Auscat')

W

WITH THE LOOKS OF AN OLD GARDEN ROSE and the vigor of a modern shrub, this is a first-rate alternative to the related pink MARY ROSE (*see page 188*), the one difference being that it is white. The most appropriate setting for it is in a cottage garden because of its old-world charm. Growth is twiggy, bushy, and uneven, and perfectly disease-resistant. The flowers will not win any prizes on the show bench, but cannot be faulted as part of a general planting plan. There is repeat-flowering and a light, barely discernible scent. Prune stems in late winter by one-half to two-thirds.

PLANT PROFILE

HEIGHT 4ft (1.2m)

SPREAD 4ft (1.2m)

TYPE Shrub

HARDINESS Z5–9

FLOWERING Summer

X | *xanthina* 'Canary Bird'

THIS NEEDS TO BE GROWN in wild or informal gardens where there is room for its arching tangle of growth. With luck there may be some later flowers, but invariably most appear in spring, making it one of the earliest roses to flower. 'Canary Bird' (which is how it is sometimes listed in catalogs) is slightly larger than the related *R. xanthina*, which also has yellow flowers in the spring. It is thorny and large, requiring plenty of space. Remove only diseased, dead, and damaged growth, and leave the old wood intact. A light trim in late winter helps to produce a balanced shape.

PLANT PROFILE

HEIGHT 10ft (3m)

SPREAD To 12ft (4m)

TYPE Shrub

HARDINESS Z5–9 H9–5

FLOWERING Late spring

xanthina f. *hugonis* Golden rose of China

X

AT 6FT (2M) HIGH AND WIDE, it produces much less intrusive, shrubby growth than the very similar *R. xanthina* 'Canary Bird', and is a better bet for more modest hedgerows and perimeter planting. The flowers are on the pale yellow side. It is sometimes known just as *R. hugonis* (Father Hugo's rose). When pruning, remove only the diseased, dead, and damaged growth, and leave the old wood intact. A minimal late-winter pruning yields a better shape, though it will never be neat.

PLANT PROFILE	
HEIGHT 6ft (2m)	
SPREAD 6ft (2m)	
TYPE Wild	
HARDINESS Z5–9	
FLOWERING Late spring	

'Zéphirine Drouhin' Thornless rose

Z

A FAVORITE SINCE 1868, this Bourbon rose has thorn-free growth, rich green leaves, and a lavish show of sweet-scented, cerise pink flowers all summer. With pruning, it forms a large shrub, but it can also be grown as a climber, reaching up to 12ft (4m) high. It can even make a hedge, and will flower (less prolifically) on a cold, shady wall. In late winter, prune the stems by one-half to two-thirds to produce a shrubby bush. Harder pruning gives fewer stems with larger flowers, while lighter pruning gives more stems with smaller blooms.

PLANT PROFILE

HEIGHT To 8ft (2.5m)

SPREAD 6ft (2m)

TYPE Old garden rose

HARDINESS Z5–9 H9–5

FLOWERING Summer to autumn

'Zigeunerknabe'

ALSO CALLED GIPSY BOY, this rose makes a small climber with strong, prickly, arching stems. It can also be grown as a large shrub when gently pruned. The flowers are superb. They have a deep, dark color highlighted by the gold stamens. The leaves may be coarse and dark green, but they are certainly disease-resistant. If you have a less-than-ideal place for a rose, this should succeed. It is sometimes listed with Bourbon roses in catalogs. In late winter, cut back stems by one-half to two-thirds, pruning harder for fewer stems with larger flowers, and more lightly for more stems with smaller blooms.

PLANT PROFILE

HEIGHT 6ft (2m)

SPREAD 4ft (1.2m)

TYPE Old garden rose

HARDINESS Z6–9 H9–6

FLOWERING Early summer

Rose suppliers

You should find many of the roses in this book at garden centers, but for more unusual varieties, try these specialist nurseries.

Almost Heaven Roses
229 Rickard Lane
Iron Station, NC 28080
(704) 732-4787
www.almostheaevenroses.com

Antique Rose Emporium
9300 Lueckmeyer Road
Brenham, TX 77833
(800) 441-0002
www.antiqueroseemporium.com

Bridges Roses
2734 Toney Road
Lawndale, NC 28090-9497
(704) 538-9412
www.bridgesroses.com

Chamblee's Rose Nursery
10926 US Highway 69 North
Tyler, TX 75706-8742
(800) 256-ROSE
www.chambleeroses.com

David Austin Roses Limited
15059 Highway 64 West
Tyler, TX 75704
(800) 328 8893
www.davidaustinroses.com

Edmunds' Roses
6235 Southwest Kahle Road
Wilsonville, OR 9707
(888) 481-7673
www.edmundsroses.com

Garden Valley Ranch Nursery
498 Pepper Road
Petaluma, CA 94952
(707) 795-0919
www.gardenvalley.com

Heirloom Roses
24062 Northeast Riverside Drive
St. Paul, OR 97137
(503) 538-1576
www.heirloomroses.com

Jackson and Perkins
1 Rose Lane
Medford, OR 97501
(877) 322-2300
www.jacksonandperkins.com

Melrose Plantation
854 Pinkardsville Road
Lancaster, VA 22503
(800) 711-4620
www.melroseplantation.com

Michaels Premier Roses
9759 Elder Creek Road
Sacramento, CA 95829
(866) 352-ROSE
www.michaelsrose.com

Nor'east Miniature Roses, Inc.
P.O. Box 307
Rowley, MA 01969
(800) 426-6485
www.noreast-miniroses.com

Orion Farm
4186 75th Street Southwest
Waverly, MN 55390
(800) 558-4180
www.orionfarm.com

Petaluma Rose Company
581 Gossage Avenue
Petaluma, CA 94952
(877) 738-2586
www.petrose.com

Regan Nursery
4268 Decoto Road
Fremont, CA 94558
(800) 249-4680
www.regannursery.com

Rose Hill Gardens
P.O. Box 5490
Santa Barbara, CA 93150
(805) 684-7702
www.rhg.com

Roses of Yesterday and Today
803 Brown's Valley Road
Corralitos, CA 95076
(831) 728-1901
www.rosesofyesterday.com

Sam Kedem Nursery
Town & Country Roses
12414 191st Street East
Hastings, MN 55033
(877) 340-2304

Sexton Nurseries Ltd.
10076 US Highway 69 North
Tyler, TX 75706-8739
(800) 527-8631
www.sextonnurseries.com

The Uncommon Rose
3333 Southwest Brooklane Drive
Corvallis, OR 97333
(541) 753-8871
www.uncommonrose.com

Vintage Gardens Antique Roses
2833 Old Gravenstein Highway South
Sebastopol, CA 95472
(707) 829-2035
www.vintagegardens.com

Wisconsin Roses
7939 31st Avenue
Kenosha, WI 53142-4617
(262) 358-1298
www.wiroses.com

The publisher would like to thank the following for their kind permission to reproduce their photographs:

a=above; c=center; b=below; l=left; r=right; t=top

21: Photos Horticultural; **27:** Roger Smith/DK; **44:** Roger Smith/DK; **53:** Roger Smith/DK; **56:** (both) Roger Smith/DK; **57:** Photos Horticultural; **69:** Garden Picture Library/David Askham; **83:** Roger Smith/DK; **87:** Photos Horticultural; **114:** Photos Horticultural; **118:** Roger Smith/DK; **126:** Roger Smith/DK; **154:** Photos Horticultural; **159:** Garden Picture Library/David Askhan; **160:** Roger Smith/DK; **166:** Roger Smith/DK; **169:** Clive Nichols; **181:** Garden and Wildlife Matters/J.Vere Brown; **182:** Garden and Wildlife Matters/Steffie Shields; **194:** Garden Picture Library/ Elizabeth Crowe; **200:** Garden and Wildlife Matters/Steffie Shields; **207:** Garden Picture Library/Densey Clyn; **210:** Kordes Rosen; **213:** Clive Nichols; **215:** Andrew Lawson; **219:** Garden Picture Library/Laslo Puskas; **235:** Photos Horticultural; **253:** (both) Roger Smith/DK; **254:** (both) Roger Smith/DK; **260:** Roger Smith/DK; **264:** Roger Smith/DK; **269:** Photos Horticultural; **275:** Roger Smith/DK; **279:** Roger Smith/DK; **300:** Roger Smith/DK; **302:** (main) Roger Smith/DK; **303:** Roger Smith/DK; **304:** Garden and Wildlife Matters; **305:** Garden Picture Library/Brigitte Thomas; **307:** Clive Nichols; **313:** Andrew Lawson.

All other images © Dorling Kindersley.

For further information see:
www.dkimages.com